FANDOM AS CLASSROOM PRACTICE

FANDOM & CULTURE
Katherine Larsen and Paul Booth, series editors

University of Iowa Press, Iowa City 52242
Copyright © 2018 by the University of Iowa Press
www.uipress.uiowa.edu
Printed in the United States of America

Design by Kristina Kachele Design, llc

No part of this book may be reproduced or used in any form or by any means without permission in writing from the publisher. All reasonable steps have been taken to contact copyright holders of material used in this book. The publisher would be pleased to make suitable arrangements with any whom it has not been possible to reach.

The University of Iowa Press is a member of Green Press Initiative and is committed to preserving natural resources.

Printed on acid-free paper

Library of Congress Cataloging-in-Publication Data
Names: Howell, Katherine Anderson, 1981– editor.
Title: Fandom in the classroom practice / edited by Katherine Anderson Howell.
Description: Iowa City : University of Iowa Press, [2018] | Series: Fandom & Culture | Includes bibliographical references and index.
Identifiers: LCCN 2017040591 (print) | LCCN 2017060665 (ebook) |
ISBN 9781609385682 (ebk) | ISBN 9781609385675 (pbk. : acid-free paper)
Subjects: LCSH: Education—Social aspects. | Popular culture—Study and teaching. | Mass media in education. | Fans (Persons)
Classification: LCC LC191 (ebook) | LCC LC191 .F27 2018 (print) | DDC 306.43—dc23
LC record available at https://lccn.loc.gov/2017040591

FANDOM AS CLASSROOM PRACTICE

A TEACHING GUIDE

Edited by
KATHERINE ANDERSON HOWELL

UNIVERSITY OF IOWA PRESS,
IOWA CITY

CONTENTS

Acknowledgments vii

INTRODUCTION. Invitation: Remix Pedagogy in the Fandom Classroom
Katherine Anderson Howell 1

CHAPTER 1. Adaptation as Analysis: Creative Work in an English Classroom
Anna Smol 17

CHAPTER 2. Becoming a Subcreator: Response to "Studies in Medievalism: Tolkien and Myth-Making"
Rebecca Power 32

CHAPTER 3. Researching the Shawshank Trail: Fan Pilgrimage and Service Learning
Maura Grady, Richard J. "Robby" Roberson Jr., and Erika Gallion 35

CHAPTER 4. Reblog, Like, and Freewrite: Online Blogging Spaces in the Composition Classroom
Leslie Leonard and Lee Hibbard 47

CHAPTER 5. Using Tumblr in the Classroom: Reflections on EH101S
Lingzi Yuan and Yixian Yang 67

CHAPTER 6. Fan Activities in Online University Education
Mattias Aronsson, Anneli Fjordevik, and Hiroko Inose 70

CHAPTER 7. Teaching Deconstruction Using Fan Vids
Shannon K. Farley 83

CHAPTER 8. Reacting to (Re)Edits: A Student's Experience with Vids
John Sanders 93

CHAPTER 9.	"You Do Realize *The Lion King* Is Set in Africa, Right?": Utilizing Fan Studies to Teach about Race and Racism in the University Classroom *Rukmini Pande* 96
CHAPTER 10.	Waves of Fandom in the Fan Studies Classroom *Paul Booth* 113
CHAPTER 11.	Creation and Analysis: Response to the Fandom and Active Audiences Class *Ashlyn Keefe* 126
APPENDIX A.	Interview with Priyadharshini Seetharaman 129
APPENDIX B.	Syllabi and Course Design 137
APPENDIX C.	Assignments 147

Bibliography 153

Contributors 161

Index 167

ACKNOWLEDGMENTS

This book went from idea to reality because of the concerted support of many people. They all share my immense gratitude.

First, my thanks go to Catherine Cocks, the original editor of this volume, who first asked "Would you like to edit a book?" Her guidance, thoughtfulness, and patience have been invaluable. I am also grateful to the University of Iowa Press for its commitment to the volume and for Ranjit Arab, who shepherded the book to the finish line.

It is fair to say that this volume would not have been possible without the gentle, caring work of the teachers at Bright Start Childcare, the day care center at which both of my children spent time during the writing and editing of this book. My academic labors are not possible without these teachers' labors. Thank you to Evelyn Garcia, Omelia Molina, Joselyn Castellanos, Ana Lopez, Honorata De Jesus, Ileana Torres, Anna Liza Abad, Walime Kontou Djeri, Dodji Shalley, Veronica Wright, and Marcia St. Hilaire-Finn.

Thank you to the University Writing Program at George Washington University, which supports the research pursuits of its adjuncts, especially Rachel Riedner, Zachary Wolfe, Sandra Freidman, and Heather Schell. Thank you to my office mates through the creation of this volume, including Brian Fitzpatrick, Edward Helfers, and Allison Sparks. Sorry I talk to myself when I write! Thank you to the students who challenged me and did amazing, creative work in my class, especially Brianna Gardner and Christiana Miller. Thank you to Joseph Fisher, who asked key questions. Thank you to Susan McMenamin, the director of Disability Support Services at George Washington University, who gave me the space to finish this volume as I moved from faculty to staff.

Thank you to my husband, John Eric Howell, for his support, and to my children, Luke and Samuel Howell, for not mashing the wrong keys on the keyboard and erasing the manuscript. I love you all.

Finally, I am deeply grateful for the friendship and mentorship of Katherine Larsen, my colleague at George Washington University. Her guidance and expertise have shaped my work in countless ways. Kathy set me down the remix path and has been a tireless sounding board ever since I first darkened her office door looking for a particular article. This book is dedicated to her.

INTRODUCTION

Invitation: Remix Pedagogy in the Fandom Classroom

Katherine Anderson Howell

> But then, as we went through the whole writing process and learned how to choose a topic and figure out what we were interested in, I realized I could explore the relationship.
> —Priyadharshini Seetharaman

As fan studies grows as a discipline—testing its ethical and disciplinary boundaries, considering the role of the acafan, and expanding and blurring its definitions of fandom—teaching of and with fandom is growing in prominence. Teaching fandom, or teaching the discipline of fan studies, implicitly involves teaching the methods that fans use when they respond to media texts as well as teaching the ways that fan scholars explore and analyze fans and fandom. Instructors of all disciplines are taking teaching lessons from fans: the ways that fans create can provide models for students in the academic classroom.

Stedman (2012, 108) describes the interactions between fan creations (videos, music, and fan fiction) and the audience for such art as "becom[ing] inherently more dialogic, responsive, and messy." The audience—"primarily other members of the same [fan] community—have already formed opinions about the . . . original texts" and respond to the new creation in ways informed by that text, learning as they do to find the "subgroups of opinions" in the community. The connections to academic disciplines and their own internal conversations may be clear, but it is important not to overlook the parallels to the classroom. Students in a given course form opinions about the course readings and then respond to one another in classroom conversations based on those opinions. Fan creations and communities provide a way to navigate and encourage messy classroom dialogue.

Stedman's study of fans focuses on their composition methods and on the creativity of their work: "in the wider culture, creativity that is obviously based on earlier work is often derided as less meaningful than work seen as 'wholly original.'" However, as Stedman points out, serious work goes into creating this art: the development of community ethics and a sense of authorship and ownership over their own creations; the use of rhetorical principles necessary to nearly any act of composition (genre, audience, and purpose); research driven by excitement and curiosity; the drive to find new possibilities and skills; and the capacity to critique culture (2012, 112–17). These are the kinds of things we mean when we talk about teaching fandom, or teaching using fan methods.

In cultures saturated with media, fans authorize themselves to critically respond and engage with their chosen texts; they do not rely on the authority of the classroom, a theory, or a degree to open the door for their response. Jenkins (2010) describes this as an act of citizenship, and like many other kinds of citizenship (e.g., activism, public writing, community contribution, and collaboration), fan methods can authorize postsecondary students to respond and engage in an academic world saturated with gatekeeping, jargon, and required curricula. Particularly since they transform their source material, fan methods of creating offer students a way to think about using research to build their own ideas.

We don't presume that our students will be fans or will understand fans. Geraghty (2012) asserts that regardless of whatever exposure students may have to interactive online communities, they may "continue to regard similar fan practices and uses of technology as being somehow inconsequential, geeky, and childish" (162). He argues, however, that "students who are wary of studying fandom and see themselves as separate from it are ultimately as much a part of participatory culture as any diehard fan" (163). Students in fan studies classes, and classes that use fan methods, may resist also because they, like most students, "do not fully engage with the scholarship" and are also uninitiated into fandom concepts (166). This double gap can be difficult to bridge, but not more so than any other kind of knowledge leap. Geraghty suggests that teachers support students by giving them agency, letting them "find their own way through the material, finding their own opinion and how to voice it" (168). Ironically, even as a fandom classroom can create a double gap for students, it can also equip them to bridge it by authorizing them to play with the material they study.

Of course, it is just as important to acknowledge that students come into the classroom with a range of experience. The active fan may eagerly grasp the concepts but resist the kinds of analysis that the classroom asks of them. They may also resist bringing fan practices into the classroom, believing this to be a level of scrutiny inappropriate for fan works and communities. They may see this kind of classroom as what I have previously called "violations of ... fannish ... norms" (Anderson Howell 2016, 326). The tension that exists in fan studies among research subject, academic method, and pleasurable engagement is difficult to fully solve, and that tension may be why many of us in this book don't bring our own fan works into our classrooms. We create classrooms that seek to use fan methods but that also must meet departmental expectations of learning objectives. We must make our classroom work rigorous in ways that fan communities are not required to; this is not to suggest that fan creators are unanalytical or unintellectual, for we know that not to be true. This is instead a strategy for forging a discipline, performing academically in order to be taken seriously, to get tenure, and to teach the classes we want.

Of course, the disconnect between the fan practices the authors in this volume engage in and the teaching the authors do could also be a way of both protecting our own pleasures (perhaps because exposing them makes us vulnerable, but also perhaps because we seek a boundary between ourselves and our students that we would not seek with fellow fans). Fans know this desire for protection well, for they make it clear to fan scholars who are establishing research ethics that they fear ridicule and exposure (Nielsen 2016, 245–46).

The chapters in this collection, and the classrooms from which they are born, view fan practices as vast: from image making to vidding, from Tumblr community participation to textual adaptation, from pilgrimage to scanlation, the fan-made scanning, translation, and editing of comics from one language to another. These chapters "translate" fan practices into more formalized fan pedagogy. Based in different disciplines, these classrooms have different focuses and use different language to describe what happens within them. Whether we frame our classrooms as remix spaces, affinity spaces, or fandom classrooms, we are all drawing from the same understanding of how students, instructors, and fans are connected. We use this understanding to create classrooms in which students can respond to, adapt, and resist canonical knowledge. Our various practices are drawn from the wide array of informal fan activities. What connects all these classroom practices together is a united pedagogical question, which Stedman (2012, 114) frames as "inventional research": "What could I *do* with this?"

According to Lessig (2008), remix creates two profound goods: community and education (77). The read-write culture (28) that allows remix "asks something more of the audience. It is offered as a draft. It invites a response" (85). The participation of an audience cocreates a culture and transforms a media text. The engagement of students in academic classrooms can lead to the cocreation of classroom culture and to a transformation of not only the students' work but also their approach to learning.

Thus, the remix classroom offers students an education with an expectation of responsibility, and in doing so it affords its students respect (Lessig 2008, 86): we expect them to ask "What could I *do* with this?" and to actively engage in the course. We also respect what they add and ask them to respect themselves and their classroom work as well. Jenkins (2010) frames this kind of respect in popular culture terms, arguing that "Peter Parker [Spiderman] belongs to a society where adults and young people relate as equals," thus giving him the ability to take risks supported by an adult rather than be limited by adult intrusion.

Of course, in order to engage young people, adults in the academic community rely on a very different sense of training or teaching than the fan community does. In academia, although there are multitudes of pedagogies and classroom types, most new students are placed in entry-level classrooms that run the risk of positioning them as recipients of a canon of knowledge. Fandom, however, operates in such a way that "'newbies,' or novices, and experts share the activities and participate in the same space." The new fan does not need to be "scaffolded into legitimate participation through . . . interactions with masters" (Black 2008a, 39).

Black (2008a, 25) draws on Homi Bhaba's "third space" as a way to understand the fandom affinity space: "a convergence of sorts where diverse mindsets, perspectives, and materialities can come together and be articulated into new interconnected and hybrid frames of mind." The fandom affinity space offers immediate entrance to this convergence; while apprenticeships, growth, and learning will occur, the novice fan can also cocreate the fandom community along with the long-term fan. It is important to resist idealizing fan communities, however. As Rukmini Pande will point out in chapter 9, there are limits to the inclusion of fan communities.

Although both the fandom affinity space and the academic classroom can offer barriers to participation in the form of unspoken rules, community norms, or open prejudice, the fandom space also gives an implicit welcome to novices that the academic classroom does not always offer. Classrooms that develop affinity, or remix (Stedman 2012) cultures by employing fan practices invite students to respond, to engage in academic discourse, and to invest more of themselves into their education, with immense potential benefit. As I have argued elsewhere, "Asking students to think like fans may challenge their perception of fandom, but it also challenges their perception of scholarship. Both, rather than consuming passively in isolation, produce in community- and discourse-centered engagement with texts" (Anderson Howell 2014, 11).

THE AFFINITY CLASSROOM

So I had to find something that I needed from the book. That's kind of how it works with science: you don't just try to find a cure to something, or you don't try to find some method because you just need to find a method. You find it, you go and look for it because you have an interest in finding a better way to optimize something, or you have an interest in finding a way to compress images better and transport them better.
—*Priyadharshini Seetharaman*

Of course, this raises the question, what is a community, be it fan or discourse based? Busse and Hellekson (2012) offer useful ways to think about both. They claim that fans "consider themselves part of a closed subculture" with specific guiding principles (46). This would suggest that the borders of fan communities are impermeable; however, Busse and Hellekson also offer that fan blogs are "communicative spaces" where "lengthy, ongoing conversations" take place and make use of "specific assumed awareness of the writer's position and tone" (48). This suggests that within the boundaries of a fan community, discourse continues in much the same manner as it does in academia: with guiding principles that depend on the space (blog, journal, conference, or discipline) in which the conversation takes place.

Busse and Hellekson (2006) make explicit the similar functions of discourse, both fan and academic. By discourse I mean a continuing conversation on a given topic, academic or otherwise: "The act of performing fandom parallels the act of performing academia. Both rely on dialogue, community, and intertexuality" (25). On this foundation I base a loose definition of *fan community*: a group of people who share similar fannish concerns and participate in similar fannish practices. This group, while perhaps "fragmented and fragmentary" (8), has the ultimate purpose of pursuing and continuing the fandom. The members of the community may have relationships with one another, but their most meaningful relationship is with the fandom.

An affinity, fandom, or remix classroom has some distinct and important differences from fandom space. Fandom space has the expectation that participants in the space have the strong relationship with the fandom or the media text that generates the fan response. The classroom has a wide range of expectations for why participants in the space are involved: curriculum requirements, relationship to majors and degrees, scheduling, and genuine interest are all reasonable expectations of a student. Thus, the classroom affinity space transforms the most meaningful relationship: instead of the fan's connection with the fandom, the student is connected with the institution or the degree. In a practical way, the student in the remix classroom has the most meaningful relationship with the idea of success in the course.

Of course, students may also have meaningful relationships with the course topics; many remix classrooms strive to create meaningful personal relationships within the classroom community. More advanced students—students who are not, in fact, academic novices—can find meaningful community that addresses both the practical academic need and the relational affinity need within the remix classroom.

Stedman (2012) argues that the remix classroom blends "text-centered approaches, focused on analysis of existing work" with "practice-centered" and "composer-centered approaches" that "allow playful experimentation and . . . amateurs to learn about the detailed choices composers actually make when composing" (107). He sets out actions that the "Remix Literate Composer" takes, including "[insisting] on the creativity and inherent worth" of remix, being "community- and collaboration-minded" and "[searching] widely for inspiration" (119). Students in a remix classroom participate in what Lessig (2008, 56) calls "an essential act of RW [or read-write] creativity." They write back to canonical knowledge, thus creating the possibility of changing or challenging that knowledge.

The remix classroom attempts to empower students to enter academic culture or to grow as participants in it, as well as to resist cultural elements that can dismiss student contributions. Duffett (2015, 3) argues that this is a central tenet of fan studies, claiming that "the framing logic of much post-Fiskean 'transformative works' scholarship is simple: attention to the right fan practices can help restore a sense of empowerment, resistance, literacy, and humanity to fan identities." Thus, regardless of the disciplinary focus of the classroom, remix offers students literacy and value in their class work, as well as citizenship.

When we invite our students to engage in a remix classroom, we are asking them to look at the class and ask what they can do with it. We invite them to participate in their education, to talk back to experts and authorities, and to shape the discourse themselves. We frame teaching and learning as actions, practices to be done, not lessons to be consumed.

Of course, creating a remix classroom also requires thoughtfulness on our, the instructors', part. The chapters in this volume come from instructors who have carefully constructed remix courses and implemented fan practices in their classrooms. They have done so with an eye not only to respect for students but also to respect for fans. Thus, this volume has a dual focus: praxis and response. Each chapter is produced by a remix instructor, and each has some form of student response, engagement, or data. The instructors have focused on providing a road map for how to successfully use fandom studies and fan practices in the classroom. You will find in these chapters practical, specific guidelines, supported with methodology, about assignment design, teaching practices, and classroom setup. The student responses will give you a sense of what students specifically gained from each course. Example syllabi are available in appendix B, and sample assignments are in appendix C.

LISTENING TO STUDENTS

The course in general just taught me how to think, which I think is probably the most important thing that it could teach you. And it taught me how to think—this going to sound so cliché—but think outside the box, how to approach a problem from different angles. It doesn't have to have a direct link, but something that you find in some other researchers' work can help you find a method to explore what you're exploring.
—Priyadharshini Seetharaman

As instructors invested in our students' progress, we often hear theoretical and practical pedagogical advice from our colleagues and peers. We very rarely hear about our pedagogy or its results from our students, which seems to be impractical and defeatist. Aside from the much maligned student evaluation, or the occasional reflection piece, how do we determine the success of our teaching strategies? How can we determine whether the practices we so passionately endorse and enthusiastically prepare are actually working? Grades? Perhaps, but these are not a precise measure. Improvement over the semester? Again, this is largely determined by our view and what we see in our students.

Hearing from the students presented in this volume allows us a glimpse into the successes, and sometimes failures, of our classroom work. These students examine the course they took and present to us an invaluable consideration: How are our students actually participating in our courses? What is moving forward? What needs work?

The student voices presented here range from coauthors to anonymous survey respondents, but they are present and valued in every work. Thus, this volume does not rely solely on an instructor's perceptions of student work or on evaluations as mere data but rather values students as coscholars and as cocreators of the classroom. The student authors in this volume include language learners discussing the practical ways that fan-based pedagogy affected their coursework, students embarking on larger scholarly pursuits based in their fan studies, and nontraditional students who have applied the fan practices from the classroom to their daily experiences. Of course, those students whose written work is published here are self-selected; they are students who desire to respond to the course, and they mostly do so positively. The chapters dealing with student evaluation data show that the practice of a fandom pedagogy correlates with instructors valuing their students' input. Even as students in classrooms that embrace fandom pedagogies react in mixed ways, remix instructors analyze these reactions critically. These instructors take student feedback seriously, because fan practices in the classroom are centered on the student. Thus, even in classes with mixed feedback, students seem to gain from a pedagogical approach that incorporates remix practices.

Black (2008a, 33) argues for the value of fan fiction to education: "Fan fiction authors . . . are learning to write in globally networked, pluralistic arenas where the convergence of different modes of representation, media, texts, languages, literacies, and perspectives is commonplace." The multimodal, multidisciplinary, audience-centered kinds of writing done by fan writers online enhances fans' learning of key literacy, critical thinking, and analytical skills, which instructors often strive for. Jenkins (2006a) offers the example of Heather Lawyer and the "informal pedagogy that emerged within the *Harry Potter* fan community" (177). This informal pedagogy creates a "jointly produced fantasy" (185) in which participants interact in ways that foreground the imaginative and play aspects of learning.

More recently, Jenkins (2010) has argued for the social and educational value of playing with, or remixing, popular culture to produce or resist larger political ideas. In his TED talk, Jenkins points out that rather than embracing media and technologies that open space for play, many schools cut off access to them. The implication is that social media and open access sources like YouTube and Wikipedia do not present opportunities for the kinds of learning that schools value: authoritative, top-down, or what Lessig (2008, 28) might call read-only: "less practiced in . . . amateur creativity." Black (2008a, 33) reinforces this critique of "classrooms where peer interaction is confined to a largely homogenous group," arguing that such classrooms "offer little room for student innovation, . . . for writing outside the margins[, and for] individuals to use language and other mediating systems to . . . construct and enact . . . identities." The remix classroom offers both instructor and student space to talk back to the ideological systems that rely on and reproduce canonical knowledge.

Jenkins (2006a, 185) suggests that participation in the playful activities that make up "convergence culture" involve values that fan scholars repeatedly identify as skills that are valued in academic work and that connect the academia with the fandom sphere: collaboration within community, the creation and discussion of moral frameworks, the following of research trails, interpretation of cultural artifacts, and consideration of an audience. Playful learning creates space for self-positioning, self-identification, and experimentation that leads to new knowledge and interpretations. The remix classroom, as described in the following chapters, strives to provide opportunities for playful learning within the classroom structure.

SCHOLARLY UNDERSTANDING OF FANDOM

I think adaptation is okay.
—Priyadharshini Seetharaman

Gray, Harrington, and Sandvoss (2007, 1) outline a history of fan studies scholarship (in this book, Booth adds to their work). The first generation is the "Fandom Is Beautiful" scholarly attitude. Scholars from John Fiske to Henry Jenkins, they point out, see fandom as "a collective strategy, a communal effort to form interpretive communities that in their subcultural cohesion evaded the preferred and intended meanings" of those who held cultural or copyright power. Hills (2002, 65) offers a critique of Fiskean fan scholarship, suggesting that a cultural studies understanding of "the fan" results in a "partial and limited examination" of fan practices.

A second wave of fan scholarship drew on the work of Bourdieu, and "highlighted the replication of social and cultural hierarchies" in order to demonstrate that "the interpretive communities of fandom . . . are embedded in the existing economic, social, and cultural status quo" (Gray et al.

2007, 6). Appropriately, Gray, Sandvoss, and Harrington label this wave "Fans in the Mainstream." Hills (2002, 47) again points to the limits of this kind of hierarchical work, noting that it "treats all social relations as if they are economic." In fact, fans often resist economic interpretations.

The third wave of scholarship is "Fandom and Modernity," which "explored the *intra*personal pleasures and motivations among fans" (Gray et al. 2007, 8). The audience is a central concern here. And as Hills (2002, 112) points out, pleasure "is not always caught up in a . . . set of cultural boundaries, but may instead imaginatively create its own set of boundaries." Fan play should not be viewed simply as boundary-crossing but instead as simultaneously rejecting preset cultural expectations and developing new ones.

Jenkins (2010) argues that "just as in a hunting society, we play with bows and arrows, in an information society, we play with information; in a mediated culture, we play with media and that play, in fact, becomes a powerful form of teaching." Thus, play in fan studies should not be regarded as empty action but as complex engagement with purpose and potential.

Hills (2002, 182) argues that fan cultures undergo an "*essentially contradictory process*" through which fan cult(ures) "challenge and intensify commodification"; "display self-reflexivity"; "function as 'interpretive communities' while providing a shared cultural space for intensely private sentiments and attachments"; and "construct hierarchical forms of internal and external cultural distinction." These inherent contradictions in the way fans operate as well as the way that fan studies scholars understand fan activity point to a kind of scholarly diversity that leads to innovation and can offer our students innovative ways to think about what they produce in a classroom space.

If we aspire to the authorizing and perceived rigor of the university as well as to the decentralizing and playfulness of fannish models, then engaging with the messy contradictions of fandom, and possibly of remix, requires us to resist easy theorization of both students and fans. The chapters in this book offer multiple ways to do so, as well as ways to see what our students gain through the student responses.

REMIX CLASSROOMS

In science, you can take someone else's methods, or you can take someone else's end goal, and you can approach it from a different way. So you don't have to cure cancer, or you don't have to cure cancer with this one particular drug; you can try another drug; you can try using ultrasound; you can try using all kinds of things and there's many ways to achieve that one end goal. Likewise, you don't have to use ultrasound just to see babies; you can use it as a cure; you can use it as another tool. And so when I started to realize that, I saw that you don't have to take source material, original works as is; you can take their end goal and see what is another way that they could have achieved this end goal.
—Priyadharshini Seetharaman

In chapter 1, Anna Smol explores the ways that her own fandom has affected her teaching. She uses fannish practices to trace adaptative patterns through J. R. R. Tolkien and thus to the classroom. In this frame, fan works become "another link in a chain of adaptations." Smol's course moves students from being observers of adaptations to becoming part of the adaptative process, while balancing student engagement and perception of rigor. Her students create transformations of Tolkien's texts in ways that show the permeable boundaries between the scholarly and the artistic.

In chapter 2, Smol's student responder, Rebecca Power, takes on the mantle of subcreator, a Tolkienean phrase, and places herself and her work in a history of storytellers and translators. She argues that being allowed to create and explore abstraction in the course rather than only discuss put her into a deeper conversation with the text.

Chapter 3 discusses how student researchers can help study fans and fan pilgrimages in order to benefit fans, pilgrimage sites, and the students themselves. Maura Grady, Richard J. "Robby" Roberson, and student coauthor Erika Gallion cover the practical and ethical challenges involved in surveying fans and bringing fandom studies, hospitality studies, and service learning together. Students learn how to create surveys and how to process the gathered data. More important, students learn how to pass an institutional review board's evaluation and obtain consent from survey participants. This issue of consent furthers the conversation on how academics and acafans can ethically study fans. The chapter also makes an important point about one of the meaningful reasons to study fans: in this case, doing so resulted in tangible benefits for the Shawshank Trail (the pilgrimage site) and for the visiting fans. All this points to a larger sense of connectedness:

between disciplines, between businesses and fans, and between students and the community.

In chapter 4, Leslie Leonard and Lee Hibbard discuss the possibilities opened by using Tumblr as a classroom tool. Doing so draws together the students who are familiar with writing and participating online with the students who are not. It also offers opportunities for better engagement between the teacher and the students and between the students themselves. The community environment created by both the peer-to-peer elements and the low-stakes writing assigned on Tumblr became especially important to nonnative speakers of English enrolled in the class.

Chapter 5 touches on the ways that Tumblr did become part of two students' daily life. Lingzi "Lindsey" Yuan's and Yixian Yang's curiosity about how Tumblr would be used in the classroom engaged them in the course, and their response reveals that the course used the platform in ways that mirrored their previous personal use. They reflect on several aspects of Tumblr as a classroom tool that provided them with guidance in the composition classroom and in other classes. Perhaps most important for these two Chinese students studying in the United States, writing on Tumblr using low-stakes assignments helped them gain confidence. This confidence ultimately transferred to other courses.

In chapter 6, Mattias Aronsson, Anneli Fjordevik, and Hiroko Inose propose a new way of engaging online language learners by connecting online course activities to online fan activities. They create both a fan fiction and a scanlation assignment for first-year university students. These students come to college with some oral skills, and the goal of the fannish assignments is to develop their written skills. The fan practices of fan fiction and scanlation engage online students in their learning by giving creative options to understand, translate, and extend literary works, including manga, in order to acquire language skills. Students engage in imaginative play; they critically read one another's works and provide constructive peer review.

Because of the nature of online learning, the student response to this chapter takes the form of analysis of evaluations and student feedback. The authors mine the data provided to them by the students to gauge not only what the students gained from the experience, such as experience with peer review, but also the kinds of obstacles the students faced in those experiences. The authors examine the range of feedback to gain a sense of what the course accomplishes for students and how it meets its goals.

In chapter 7, Shannon K. Farley examines vidding as a way to teach critical literary theory. Vidding, as a fan practice, provides a clear path for students to understand the aim of deconstructive readings: to show the unstable nature of texts. Farley uses vids as a teaching tool to show students how different kinds of critical arguments are made. She points to normative assumptions throughout the course, identifying the ways in which deconstruction, as a literary theory, intersects with other forms of criticism, as well as the ways in which fan vids make intersectional arguments by performing deconstructive analysis on the canon text.

In chapter 8, John Sanders responds to Farley's chapter by discussing the clarity that viewing different kinds of fan vids gave to his understanding of critical literary theory, especially to the concept of deconstruction. Sanders points out that viewing vids "destabilized [his] belief in [canonical] authority," and that even when this destabilization made him and his peers uncomfortable, they recognized the vid as creating a new story.

In chapter 9, Rukmini Pande begins by challenging some fan studies assumptions about fans—namely, that fan spaces are entirely welcoming and receptive spaces. She then uses actual fan responses to demonstrate how fans often whitewash characters of color and react negatively to media depictions of these characters as black or brown. Pande explores racebending, which she defines as a fan practice in which both white characters and those canonically nonwhite characters cast as white in film versions of books are reimagined as characters of color. She examines racebending in the form of "gif-sets" (graphic interchange format files) that recast or dream-cast film roles with actors of color, as a resistant fan practice. She brings this resistance into her classroom as a way of revealing students' assumptions about race and of teaching students to continue to engage with discomfort.

In chapter 10, Paul Booth asks students to discover fandom as a discipline and view their own fan practices as an object of study. Students begin by taking a historical look at fandom as a growing academic subject. They begin to see fandom as both crossing boundaries and creating connections, particularly among scholars, fans, and students. Thus, the academic subject becomes connected to the students' experiences. Students discover how a discipline evolves and are able to see fannish practices, such as slash, in the light of particular waves of the discipline, thus separating their emotional responses to such practices from a critical approach to them. They question their own relationship to fans and texts, pointing to a potential new wave in fan studies.

Chapter 11, Ashlyn Keefe's response to Booth's chapter, highlights the multiple pathways of engagement, both critical and playful, presented in the course. She remarks on the distinctions created among being a fan, consuming fan-created materials, creating one's own fan materials, and then analyzing one's creations. This multiplicity of participation heightens the blurred boundaries among fans, scholars, and students. Keefe reminds us that our students are actually all three.

CONCLUSION: REMIX AND STUDENT IDENTITY

I was frustrated. I was frustrated that I couldn't get
the answer. I wanted to find the answer.
—Priyadharshini Seetharaman

In this volume you will find chapters by instructors in a variety of university roles: tenure-track faculty, lecturers, adjuncts, university staff, and graduate students. You will find established scholars, new PhDs and MAs, and current graduate students. We study or work at universities in six countries (Canada, China, India, Spain, Sweden, and the United States) and have a wide range of disciplinary backgrounds and research interests. These include: languages, television and film studies, literature, composition, gaming, history and classics, hospitality, digital literacy, media studies, and medievalism. The chapters coincide in ways that make the international and interdisciplinary nature of fandom studies clear; this diversity of experience will demonstrate the democratizing potential of remix.

Our student responders also offer a wide range of experiences, interests, and goals. They are international exchange students, nontraditional students, and new graduate students. They are writers, researchers, poets, gamers, and fans. This range of experience speaks to the value of the fan studies classroom's openness to different disciplines and modes of scholarship.

The invitations into the more participatory classroom culture represented in this volume have a fundamentally ethical component: when our invitations are inclusive in the ways that fans have the potential to be, we democratize the classroom. Conversations about race, gender, sexuality, and disability are constant in fandom; discussing these issues frankly *is* a kind of fan practice. If we believe that the distance among scholars, fans, and students is in fact minimal, we cannot shy away from exploring the implications of our pedagogy for and with these students. Although chapter 9 is a key step, a more critical exploration of identity and diversity must take place.

If, in fact, we agree with Black's (2008a, 33) presentation of fans as creating in spaces where language, literacy, and identity are plural, then our goal in both our scholarship and our pedagogy should be to explore these pluralities. Gray-Rosendale and Birnley (2011, 218) argue that "popular culture texts are notoriously one-dimensional, oftentimes silencing or even erasing ... the realities ... of our students." They argue that the popular culture classroom must appreciate that our students can "embody" the kinds of "complex questions" raised by the pluralities that Black describes and must shape its pedagogical goals appropriately.

Fan communities can replicate or resist the one-dimensional nature of popular culture. Classrooms can as well. The remix classroom, through its invitation to write back, can offer ways to transform popular culture as multidimensional. Duffett (2015, 2–3) argues that some fan "practices 'redeem' pop culture—and its dedicated audience—through continual acts of transformation" and that these transformative actions can be done by individuals or by communities. Remix classrooms can create transformative learning communities. After all, as Jenkins (2010) argues, "If we think [participatory culture] works on an organizational level to mobilize citizenship, shouldn't we bring it into our classrooms?"

What does remix offer students who may be excluded from the discourse? If our classrooms offer invitations, how do we shape those invitations to include all our students? This volume begins to answer these questions. Theoretically, we offer an argument about why instructors might want to create remix classrooms. In addition to suggesting multiple methodologies, we show you how students have responded to the invitations we've issued, as well as why these invitations mattered and what students achieved when they accepted. Practically, we offer here several guides for how to implement a fandom-based pedagogy. There are multiple ways of issuing invitations, and in a variety of disciplines. Here we hope to show how using fan practices in our classrooms offers complements to traditional teaching that are more inclusive.

ADAPTATION AS ANALYSIS

Creative Work in an English Classroom

Anna Smol

I discovered fan fiction one day by accident. Some time after the release of Peter Jackson's film *The Fellowship of the Ring* (2001), in a scramble to find out more about his movies I came across an online discussion board that delved into all things Tolkien. My ensuing engagement with fans, both playful and serious, somehow landed me in a fan-fic site. (Who can remember the exact route through Web discussions and links when the bread crumbs have long since disappeared?) One site led to another as I read a great deal of recommended fics and metacommentaries and was impressed by the detailed knowledge of J. R. R. Tolkien's works that I found, whether the fic was offering, in Sheenagh Pugh's (2005, 19–21) terms, "more of" or "more from" the canonical story.[1] My introduction to fanworks soon expanded to include art, vidding, music, cosplay, and gaming—a transmedia extravaganza of adaptations based on the Tolkien books and/or the Jackson film trilogies based on *The Lord of the Rings* and *The Hobbit*.

Although I identified as a fan (and eventually started creating my own fan art), I could not help but also view fan works through academic lenses. As a professor of English literature and an acafan (Hills 2002), I enjoyed the quality of writing in many fics.[2] I appreciated the depth of analysis that was required to produce a good fan work; I marvelled at the dedication of fans who were so committed to their creations. And I started asking myself how I could encourage the same commitment and creative response to texts in my students that I was seeing in fans.

I teach undergraduate courses in medieval literature—in both Old English and Middle English—and a course on medievalism (the re-creation of any aspect of the Middle Ages in a later time) with a special focus on Tolkien. Inherent in these subjects are the concepts of adaptation and intertextuality. Whether discussing oral traditions and Anglo-Saxon poetry, Chaucer's "borrowings" from continental authors, or Tolkien's re-visioning of texts such as *Beowulf* or *The Battle of Maldon* in his fiction, in my classes we observe and analyze the processes and products of adaptation.

In all these courses, we find older texts erupting beyond whatever historical boundaries we might try to set: *Beowulf*, for example, in John Gardner's (1989) novel *Grendel* or in Robert Zemeckis's (2007) film; Arthurian tales in late nineteenth-century children's stories; Chaucer's *Canterbury Tales* in the contemporary poetry of Patience Agbabi (2015); lines from the Old English poem "The Wanderer" in the voice of Bernard Hill playing Theoden in Jackson's *The Two Towers* (2002). My students are encouraged to recognize in their analyses of texts such as these what Hutcheon and O'Flynn (2013, 6) call, borrowing a term from Michael Alexander, the "palimpsestuous" quality of adaptations.

Because my Tolkien course (Studies in Medievalism: Tolkien and Myth-Making) provides the greatest scope for an approach to adaptation and intertextuality, I will use it as my primary case study here. The process of studying these ideas is made easier by Tolkien's thoughts on storytelling, which establish certain concepts that open the way to thinking about a continuing tradition of adaptations. In Tolkien's seminal essay on fantasy, "On Fairy-Stories" (2008), he uses images to depict the intertextuality of all stories and the transformative potential of artists. The first image is the "Cauldron of Story," which is the soup pot into which all the elements of stories are stirred and then extracted according to the tastes of the cook (46). The second is the "Tree of Tales," related to the different branches of language families, which can be "replanted in almost any soil." Although the Tree produces leaves every year on the same pattern, "each leaf, of oak and ash and thorn, is a unique embodiment of the pattern." (66). These concepts suggest that using archetypal patterns in different variations or working with historical or mythical sources is part of the transformative power of storytelling and can be applied to any medium. In his essay Tolkien further asserts the "human right" to create. Although he frames his discussion in Christian terms—"we make in our measure and in our derivative mode, because we are made: and not only made, but made in the image and likeness of a Maker"—his claim of the human "sub-creative" faculty, as he calls it, can provide a general theoretical justification for adaptations of previous stories in original ways (66).

These are important concepts for students to handle in a Tolkien course, although the situation is further complicated by Tolkien's actual reactions to other people's works based on his writings—sometimes with approval, as in Pauline Baynes's drawings (Tolkien 1981), which are reminiscent of medieval illustrations and leave enough room for viewers to fill in the details of the story from their own imaginations (133), and at other times with strong disapproval, as in the Morton Grady Zimmerman screen treatment, which alters key elements of Tolkien's story (270–77). Abrahamson (2013) summarizes the situation this way: "While Tolkien may have been squeamish about seeing fanworks produced directly from his fiction, he supported individual reader interpretation as well as the text's ability to support various interpretations" (56), and she goes on to point out how Tolkien himself could be seen as a fan-fic writer, for example, in his retelling of the Kullervo story from *The Kalevala* (63).

Although these ideas are specific to a Tolkien course—and provide rich, challenging material to work on when thinking of adaptation, intertextuality, authorship, and fan works—the nature of our course material also involves traditional source study and literature-film adaptation, which are other avenues into the study of fan works. Tolkien always emphasizes that critics should be primarily concerned with the quality of a story instead of simply tracing its sources, an attitude that is consistent with Hutcheon and O'Flynn's (2013) approach, which eschews treating adaptations as derivative works secondary in importance to their sources; this approach has long been shared by film critics as well. All kinds of works can be included under Hutcheon and O'Flynn's (2013) three-point definition of an adaptation:

- An acknowledged transposition of a recognizable other work
- A creative *and* an interpretive act of appropriation and salvaging
- An extended intertextual engagement with the other work (8)

Viewed in this theoretical framework, fan works (such as fiction, art, video, and cosplay) become another link in a chain of adaptations—another leaf on the Tree of Tales, or another recipe from the Cauldron of Story—although it is important to note that they cannot be studied in exactly the same way as other more canonical works. Fan fiction, for example, is typically posted in online communities, and outsiders who blunder into the community to leave their critical marks or who adopt a superior subject position in relation to fandom are not welcome, as is evidenced in the recent controversy over a University of California course that attempted to study fan fiction. It is instructive to read Baker-Whitelaw's (2015) post as a first step. Becoming familiar with fan communities and making clear to students how they operate and what their expectations are is essential if fan works are to be included as course materials. If not the professor, then some of the students in the class who already identify as fans can be an invaluable resource in explaining to others the mores of their communities.

In any case, in my courses I had plenty of material to provide objects of study in various kinds of adaptations, from "professional" to "amateur," a boundary that quickly becomes blurred as we look at works such as Jackson's film trilogy (2001–2003), Bouchard's (2009) *The Hunt for Gollum*, academic essays in scholarly journals and fannish metaessays, or published illustrators and online artists' sites. As I developed my syllabi, the thought eventually occurred to me that instead of studying the process of adaptation only as observers, my students could be given the option of experiencing the process of adaptation firsthand. I could give them an opportunity to create a transformative work in any medium as a response to a text we were studying in the hope that they too would invest as much energy and creativity into the process as committed fans do. Why just study adaptations as an external observer when you can create an adaptation and experience the process, as it were, from the inside?

Some of the students who sign up for my Tolkien class already consider themselves fans of Tolkien and/or Jackson. Others acknowledge that they haven't read the books or haven't seen the movies. Some students might be heavily involved in different fandoms, others hardly at all. Whatever our starting points, by the end of the year I expect my students to be aware of the issues involved in negotiating different subject positions as academics and/ or as fans, to be able to reflect on their own position in relation to these categories, and, I hope, to partake in the play of fandom if they so choose.[3] There is the possibility of movement in understanding here for all, no matter what their starting point. In other words, I would like students to study adaptations, to create them, and to reflect on them in an informed way, especially in the context of fan studies.

I had two initial concerns about presenting students with the option of creating their own fan works. What if no one wants to do such a project? Or what if they all want to do such a project in the belief that this would be an easy assignment? For example, someone who is a skilled artist could just sketch a lovely picture of a statuesque woman in medieval garb and say that it's the elf queen Galadriel, and although that could be a beautiful picture, it might have little to do with an examination of the text or a representation of any theory connected with the course material.

My first worry about student interest was quickly dispelled. Many students eagerly embrace the option of a creative project, often because it gives them the opportunity to demonstrate some of their talents that are otherwise hidden from me as a literature instructor, such as the ability to write poetry, paint, sing, or play music. Such engagement with the course material draws out more of the whole person than we might see in our classes otherwise. Some students are eager to try new things: one student told me that she had always wanted to take a creative writing course but could never fit it into her schedule, and this project finally allowed her to experiment with writing a story for the first time in her academic career. A few students, however, daunted by the enthusiasm of others who are confident in their various artistic abilities, worry about whether there is anything that they can do. I always tell these English students that they should recognize that they already have the background to try writing a story or a poem or to do a dramatic performance, even if they are attempting this for the first time. Occasionally I will find that a student creates their own genre: I had one student who believed that she could not draw, but she wanted to create a storyboard for a dystopian film version of Tolkien's *The Lord of the Rings* set in the future. Instead of making a detailed storyboard, Shelby MacGregor (2015) photographed vignettes for her imagined film. She chose the locations, made or bought the props and costumes, and had a friend take the high-quality photographs that illustrated key moments in her potential film (figs. 1 and 2). Another student, Jessica Herritt (2013), performed what could be described as a dramatic creative movement piece. This student was not trained as a dancer, but she performed gestures and stylized movements to accompany her prerecorded reading of Tolkien's description of the corruption of elves into orcs; her performance culminated in the smearing of dark green paint all over her body as she transformed her physical being in front of our eyes.

My second concern—whether students would think that this is an easy way out of analyzing our texts and thinking about adaptation—was addressed through developing a structured sequence of steps for the project, based on ideas that I borrowed from two of my colleagues, Jeffrey MacLeod and Nick Webb, who teach art or assign arts-informed research projects. I divide the assignment into three stages, explained to my students this way (see appendix C): (1) Design: What are you planning to do? (2) Craft: How effectively did you do it? and (3) Insight: What did you learn from doing it? The whole assignment in all of its stages should be presented as early as possible in the semester, because experience has shown me that students need a long time to accomplish the first two stages successfully, and then they need time afterward to reflect adequately on the whole process.

The first stage, design, is crucial to the success of the project. In this phase

FIGURE 1 | This photograph from Shelby MacGregor's storyboard depicts characters from *The Lord of the Rings* arriving at the entrance to Mordor in a dystopian setting. MacGregor uses photographs rather than drawn storyboards to imagine the dystopian film. "The Black Gate" is courtesy of Shelby MacGregor.

FIGURE 2 | Here MacGregor's storyboard portrays a character silhouetted against a dystopian interpretation of the fires of Mordor. The image gives a sense of the style of the imagined film and how it would fit into the dystopian genre. "Mordor" is courtesy of Shelby MacGregor.

students record in a journal their research and their planning. From the beginning I emphasize that the projects must be informed by research, for our English courses at Mount Saint Vincent University require that students not only handle primary materials but also practice researching and integrating secondary sources. Many students are already familiar with process logs or research journals in other courses, and I explain that this is a similar type of assignment, only it should also include, if applicable, their ideas about and experiments with their materials along with their more conventional research. I ask students to include the date of their activity and to present in full sentences a clear account of their planning: Did they collaborate with others? What secondary sources did they consult and where did they find them: library catalog, database, library shelves, or the Web? Did they need to ask for help in finding secondary sources? What ideas from these sources might inform their project? In their planning, did they try some freewriting, brainstorming, or outlining? Depending on the nature of their project, did they create preliminary sketches, drafts, or storyboards? I emphasize that students should keep track of their dead ends as well as their discoveries—all are part of the research design process.

I have found that it is best to set two deadlines for this design log. The first occurs after several weeks so that I can ensure that the students are making adequate progress, that they are able to research their topic with appropriate sources, and that their initial plan is manageable. Enthusiasm and ambition can sometimes derail a project, as I found several years ago when I did not check on my students' progress early enough in the process: A group of students had decided to produce a film retelling the entire story of The Lord of the Rings. I thought that they were planning to produce a three-minute fan video, but by the time I realized the full scope of what they thought they could do, it was too late to advise otherwise. They spent a great deal of time (and had a lot of fun) filming, but their other course work suffered, and their project resulted in a weak adaptation that was not well-informed by adequate research or analysis.

As a result I set the second deadline: an early due date, usually within three or four weeks after the start of the semester, for part one of the design log and to enumerate clear goals, such as the following:

- Your design log at this stage should be a fairly detailed document of at least 1,500 words charting your research and creative progress.
- You should have by the end of this first part of the design process a definite idea of what your topic or creative product will be.

- You should have some ideas about what you need to do to get to the final submission (i.e., what books you still want to read; what research topics you still need to understand; what creative processes you still need to go through).
- You should include an annotated bibliography of the secondary sources you have read up to this point. Annotations should be in correct MLA style.

Even in this early phase of design planning, the students' logs give me insight into how they are engaging with the course material in a way that would not be evident if they only showed me a final copy of a research paper.

For example, Leah Phillips (2013, 1), an experienced fan-fic writer, wrote about how impressed she was in reading Tolkien's cosmology in *The Silmarillion*: "As I was reading the beginning chapters of *The Silmarillion* I was seeing the birth of an entire mythos and the world of Middle-earth. I was taken by the style of this cosmology. As an amateur writer I would absolutely love to create a cosmology and a world this complex for my own writing. I already have quite a few scraps of my own material and some concepts of what my cosmology would be." Although she eventually decided that trying something similar with her own fictional universe would be too big a task for the course project, she recorded her developing thoughts as she continued to read Tolkien's fiction: "As much as these writing ideas appeal to me, I've got an image starting to form in my mind of the two Lamps that once lit Middle-earth and the two trees of Valinor. This is still fairly conceptual, but it could incorporate ideas about light and dark or the use of colour in Tolkien's work. I don't know where this could go, but I'm quite handy with a paintbrush. This could be a more accomplishable task than writing a brand-new cosmology."

The fact that the design log asks students to record the dates of their thoughts and activities as they work toward a deadline for explaining their plans can have the desirable effect of enhancing their sense of time management. As Leah's design log (Phillips 2013) progressed, she recorded her further engagement and excitement in reading Tolkien's theoretical discussion of fantasy and art:

> Wow. I've been reading "On Fairy Stories." It's strange that I find myself disagreeing with Tolkien about painting and fantasy in imagery. He says the following on the subject: "In human art Fantasy is a thing best left to words, to true literature. In painting, for instance, the visible pre-

sentation of the fantastic image is technically too easy; the hand tends to outrun the mind, even to overthrow it" (pg 49). He does defend this reasoning in the note at the end. In the note, he argues, "Literature works from mind to mind." (pgs 77, 78). I think I get what he's saying. An artist can only produce one image and it won't be the same image that is in another reader's head. But I think that a painting, especially a more conceptual one[,] may produce the same image in two people's eyes, but it will create different thoughts, provoke different emotions, and stir different memories and meanings in those viewers' minds. I guess it's the same argument reversed. One word can produce multiple images in the mind and one image can produce multiple words in the mind.

I'm quite enjoying Tolkien's thoughts about fantasy and language especially when speaking about the leaves of trees on pages 56 and 57. I would like to incorporate all of this discussion into the concept for the painting. (4)

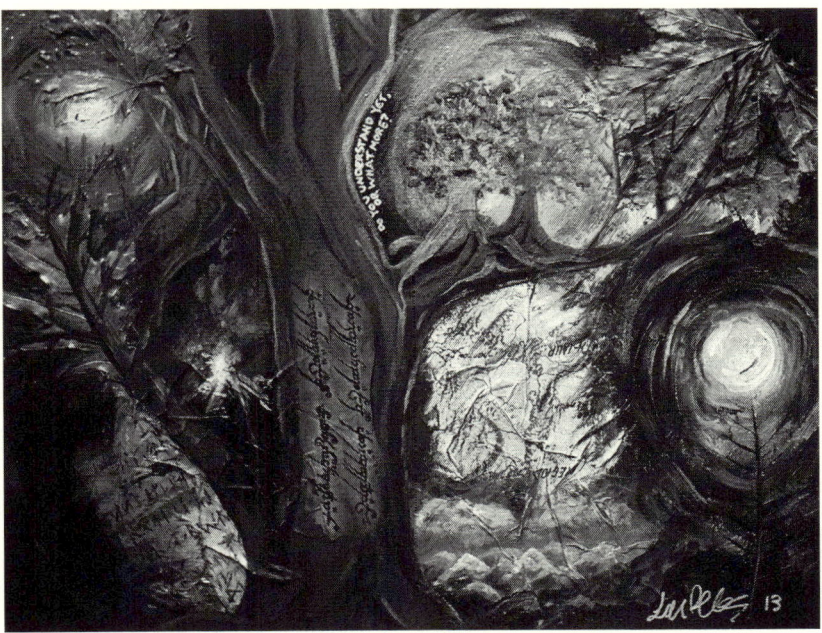

FIGURE 3 | The details of the painting "Tree of Tales" show the culmination of the design process where leaves, Elvish writing, and color reveal the connections between fantasy and art that artist Leah Phillips made from Tolkien's work. The image of the "Tree of Tales" is courtesy of Leah Phillips.

As planned, her multimedia painting incorporated concepts from Tolkien's fiction and nonfiction and responded critically to some of his ideas about art and fantasy (fig. 3).

The second and final deadline for the design log should prompt students to finish their planning with enough time to accomplish their goals. I ask students to continue the narrative of their research and creative progress and to include an element of their project design, suggesting the following goals for different types of projects:

- For art projects: A working sketch with an account of techniques to be used.
- For video projects: A storyboard of planned shots and a working script.
- For creative writing projects: A summary of the story, a list of characters, and a clear account of the style you are planning to write in, with at least one draft paragraph of the final work.
- For music projects: A clear account of the musical style and techniques to be used, as well as any lyrics that you are planning to include in your performance or recording.

These are just suggestions, of course; I usually consult individually with students about the nature of their proposed projects and what I would need to see in their final design log. Both phases of the design log assignment enable me to advise students on appropriate research for their projects. I also frequently encourage students to discuss their projects in progress with one another in case they can get good practical advice about art materials, writing tips, rehearsal spaces, video editing guidelines, and the like, as well as encouragement for their ideas. In this way the classroom can reproduce the best features of a fan community. Booth (2015a), while recognizing that fandom is certainly not a utopian space, defines the aim of "critical fandom" in a way that can also serve an important pedagogical function: "it's about how individuals comment to and react to each other in productive and respectful ways" (1.9).

In the second phase of the assignment, craft, the students present their projects to an audience. When I first tried this kind of assignment, my students asked me if they could invite others to their presentations. I expected they would ask a few friends to come along for moral support. I did not expect to see the audience filled with friends, parents, siblings, grandparents, and spouses—and this happens consistently. The students themselves, then, set the personal stakes quite high, and their pride in the demonstration of their work suggests a commitment that goes beyond a strategic concern for grades. In a small class the students can take turns presenting their projects to the whole group. In larger classes, where time constraints do not allow individual presentations to the whole class, I usually divide the students into two or three groups and set up stations in a kind of research fair. Each group takes a turn for a set amount of time arranging its projects at different stations, which the other students can visit. If the project is a poem or a short story, students can read excerpts to their audience. If the project is artwork or a video, the student can give a short introduction and then show the piece to whoever comes by. However it is accomplished, a presentation is an integral part of the project, demonstrating Coppa's (2006, 239) definition of fan fiction (and extending it to other media) as "a cultural performance that requires a live audience."

The issue of how to grade creative projects is solved by the definition of the craft stage: How effectively did you convey your design? As an English professor, I do not feel qualified to grade students as if I were an art teacher, a filmmaker, or a musician who is assessing the students' grasp of professional techniques. But I can assess the effectiveness of their projects—how well they engaged their audience—especially in light of what they expressed as their aims in their design logs. Sometimes a student project will take me far afield from what I am familiar with. For example, Amy Burke (2010) decided to do a dramatic retelling of an Old Norse poem that influenced Tolkien, "The Seeress's Prophecy"—only she decided to retell the poem in American Sign Language (ASL), which she used in her part-time job. Amy played her recording of the poem in modern English while signing in front of her audience. Even though no one else in the audience understood ASL, we could see what she was trying to achieve: an aesthetically engaging and dramatic retelling of a story in a visual language. In other words, her craft was effective in conveying her design, which was clearly expressed in her log, where she explained that she was aiming to achieve her interpretation of the poem using the fundamentals of ASL ,including "gesture, mime, and facial expressions," among other means (5). Although I could not judge how successful her translation into ASL was, I could assess, based on her signing (which truly mesmerized her audience) and her written design log that she had read her source text closely, had done research on its meaning and genre, and had applied some theories about translation and adaptation that we had studied in class to her performance.

Assessing these projects is a serious business that I am required to undertake (and I expect students to undertake their work seriously, too), but I also believe that acknowledging the play inherent in creating fan works is important in setting the right atmosphere for students to be eager to display their craft. After all, fans play with their sources, and they do it out of love of their subject—not a bad attitude to inculcate in a student working on a project. Sometimes the right atmosphere will draw out a student who would otherwise remain quiet and whose ideas and talents would be largely unacknowledged.

For example, Drew Jackson (2014) was a student who did not like participating in class discussions. Everyone in our class was somewhat surprised when Drew stood up to read his comic story based on *The Hobbit*, revealing to us his mischievous sense of humor that could adapt elements of the novel and apply the theme of a heroic adventure to a contemporary everyman. Drew explained that he wrote his story using a third-person narrator who is describing events that have already happened, as Tolkien does. The opening paragraph of Drew's story adapts Tolkien's sentence structure to introduce a present-day adventure of a young man named Brian: "In an average one-bedroom apartment there lived a man. Not a physically impressive or wealthy man, but a man who looked like someone you might see walking down the street on any given day, or in front of you in line at the bank" (4). The story recounted an improbable night on the town, including a hip-hop dance battle with a visiting group of horse jockeys from Kennebunkport, Maine (analogous to Tolkien's dwarves in the Battle of the Five Armies), and a scene with Brian's ex-girlfriend, whose Gollum-inspired riddles about "why hasn't he called" and "when can we go out for frozen yogurt again" he must answer in his attempts to avoid her (3–4).

The third and final phase of the project, insight, is a written reflection on the project and on what the student has learned in completing the process. The students have an opportunity here to revise portions of the design log if they wish to express more clearly their project aims or to develop their ideas further. They are expected to explain the thesis or focus of their project; to reflect in detail on what went well and what could have been done differently (with my assurances, of course, that expressing shortcomings will not detract from their grade if presented as thoughtful revisions); to convey how their use of secondary sources stimulated their ideas or supported their craft; and to reflect on their learning about the primary sources, the theoretical readings, or the nature of adaptations and fan works. In her final reflection, Jenny Davison (2011) reviewed her project, a sculpture of the Doors of Durin (fig. 4), for which she carefully modeled trees imitating Tolkien's painted trees, copied his inscription on the doors, added details to the sculpture based on Tolkien's textual descriptions, and acknowledged the transmedia influence of Jackson's film version of the scene. Jenny described her research into Tolkien's artwork and the symbolism of trees in his various stories. She recounted her attempts (successful in the end) to figure out how to make the inscription on her sculpture light up in the dark, just as in Tolkien's story it appears only under moonlight. Jenny's thinking about her piece involved applying knowledge she had gained in an astronomy course, thus connecting previous knowledge to her creative problem. She was further delighted when she came across a couple of scientists who have written about Tolkien's interest in astronomy, leading her to the discovery of what she called "science fandom": "my train of thought reflects the kind of thinking inherent in science fandom: How might this actually happen? How could it be true?" (10).

In a different kind of reflection, Rebecca Power (2014) reviewed her interest in Tolkien's frequently repeated story of the romantic couple Beren and Lúthien: "I wanted to reproduce the story of Beren and Lúthien due to its significance to Tolkien, to participate in enhancing its mythology by pro-

FIGURE 4 | The "Doors of Durin Tree" sculpture demonstrates how interdisciplinary research interacts with creative work. Using astronomy, history, and primary source research, Jenny Davison sculpted this work, which also lights up as Tolkien's doors do. The image of the sculpture "Doors of Durin Tree" is courtesy of Jenny Davison.

viding another retelling of the story, and to understand the process of writing in alliterative meter" (5). As a fairly experienced creative writer, Rebecca decided to try her hand at writing in Old English–style alliterative meter because she found alliteration to be an appealing poetic effect. In reflecting on her research and her rendering of a scene from the Beren and Lúthien story, she realized that she had not always adhered as strictly to the rules of alliterative meter as Tolkien had. Her account illustrates the effectiveness of hands-on learning: "I learned very quickly that Modern English has more syllables than Old English, and that many of my sentences were being dictated by the alliteration, rather than the alliteration enhancing what I had to say. After [I] produc[ed] and revis[ed] a few drafts, the alliteration became easier and the sentences felt more natural. Now that I have presented my reproduction of Beren and Lúthien, I can see the strong aspects of my version, and notice that my own particular style and voice have slowly become apparent" (5–6). In these reflections, students should always be encouraged to express their difficulties in achieving their goals, because this clarifies their learning both for themselves and for their instructor.

Rebecca's experience is one example of how creating a fanwork can lead to impressive engagement with the subject. Not satisfied with her final experiments with the form in my Tolkien class, she decided to dedicate a full year to researching an honors thesis on medieval and modern uses of alliterative meter and on Tolkien's Beren and Lúthien stories and to writing her own re-creation of more of the story in correct alliterative meter. Her Beren and Lúthien poem is a fan-fic piece, and like most good fan works, it is based on a close analysis of her source material. As Rebecca indicated in her insight reflection, she wanted to enhance Tolkien's mythology by retelling one of his stories; she understood, in Tolkien's terms, that she was adding another leaf to the Tree of Tales.

Incorporating fan studies and fannish practices in my classes has fired up some of that "fannish ardor" that Booth (2015a) believes can only benefit our educational system (1.1). He lists a number of writers who have discussed the advantages of including fan studies in the classroom (3.5), but his summary of "fan-based modes of critical thinking" as "Creative thinking. Collaboration. Aesthetic experience" (3.2) provides probably one of the best and most succinct arguments for including fan studies in the English literature classroom.

NOTES FOR CHAPTER 1

1. Sheenagh Pugh describes these two general motives for the writing of fan fiction. On the one hand, fans might want *more of* a story, so they write further episodes, such as fans did after Arthur Conan Doyle's death to continue writing Sherlock Holmes stories. On the other hand, fans sometimes want a story to develop in different ways; they want *more from* the story, such as better-developed relationships or more overt emotions, and this can also be the impetus for their fan fiction. My students can follow either motivation in their own work.

2. In his book *Fan Cultures*, Matt Hills discusses the complexities in identifying as an academic fan (or acafan), in which the academic side is primary, or as a fan scholar, someone who identifies primarily as a fan who performs scholarly work. The term *acafan* has been widely used, certainly made popular by noted media critic Henry Jenkins (n.d.) in his blog, *Confessions of an Aca-Fan*, where he defines the term as "a hybrid creature which is part fan and part academic." Jenkins shares the goal expressed by many critics, such as Matt Hills, Karen Hellekson, and Kristina Busse, to find a way to bridge their fan and academic sides. Hellekson and Busse (2006, 8), for example, emphasize "fandom's communal spirit" and express their aim to "use our fannish knowledge and values and apply them to academic practices."

3. I usually allow students to choose a more conventional research paper instead of a creative project. By the time students get to my senior-level courses, they are fairly well versed in writing academic papers, but my assignment structure makes them look at their essays in a new light, as carefully designed and crafted pieces of writing—works of creative art in themselves—that will be presented to an audience and that will be the subject of their review and reflection in the final stage. Students who opt to write an academic essay must follow the three stages of the assignment: design, craft, and insight.

BECOMING A SUBCREATOR

Response to "Studies in Medievalism: Tolkien and Myth-Making"

Rebecca Power

Dr. Anna Smol's course in medievalism has influenced me to become what J. R. R. Tolkien called a subcreator: a creator of myths and worlds through the use of language. The opportunity to be creative and provide my own adaptations of various stories encouraged me to take risks and pursue my interests within academia. This course changed the future of my academic career, allowing me to rediscover creativity in my academic work and be fearless in my academic endeavors. By becoming a subcreator I was inspired to do more than discuss my interests, and instead I began to actually pursue them; we were given the opportunity to try out specific artistic forms by writing or painting them, instead of solely writing essays about them. From the opportunities this course provided, I have been more open in my other courses to explore more creative and abstract ideas.

The study of Old English and Old Norse stories introduced us to different poetic forms and modes of storytelling, looking at translated versions while also discussing the original form. The translations themselves were also a point of interest; it was our first look at how these texts were being adapted, since the translators had to make the decision to attempt to adhere to form as well as content, or to provide the most direct translation of the text. As the course went on, we were able to see patterns throughout the stories and realize how interlaced the texts were with one another to create a mythology. Each writer and translator was a subcreator, contributing to and enhancing mythologies through their careful use of language.

Combining these elements of adaptation and mythology with the works of Tolkien, the course connected these old works with modern texts, demonstrating how adaptation plays an important role within literature. Tolkien was a great example of this, since he provided adaptations of these Old

English and Old Norse stories through translations and references within his own work. Tolkien also reproduced his own stories numerous times in various forms and was himself a subcreator, through the production and reproduction of his stories as well as by allowing various characters to create through the use of language within his stories.

Through learning about adaptation I became interested in Tolkien's Beren and Lúthien story. To demonstrate my newfound interest, I used a creative project we were given that allowed us to become part of the ongoing conversation that adaptation creates. After researching Tolkien's descriptions of Beren and Lúthien to discover their likeness, as well as his descriptions of color in clothing and landscape to determine how Tolkien presented the world around them (mainly in primary colors), I painted Beren and Lúthien. I also incorporated a portion of a poem Tolkien wrote about Beren and Lúthien and represented it in one of his Elvish scripts. This painting also provided me with an opportunity to choose a scene I was affected by and wanted to represent.

As a subcreator I was able to join in a direct conversation with the text through adaptation, making it easier for me to understand the content and appreciate the form. This course allowed me to provide multiple adaptations of the works that we were learning about through painting and poetry, and this level of involvement assisted in heightening my engagement with the text, both emotionally and intellectually. More than just reading the text and discussing the content, we discussed the form and mode of production as well as how else it could be represented through adaptation.

During the course we also looked at examples of poetry, including Old English alliterative meter. The structure of the meter intrigued me, because it is a form of poetry made for the English language that values alliteration rather than rhyme. For my second project, I decided to use this alliterative form to write a portion of the Beren and Lúthien story, which proved to be both challenging and rewarding. By writing in this form, I was able to more fully understand its intricacies, admire those who wrote using it, and gain an appreciation for oral poetry and storytelling by actively engaging in its production and presentation.

Each creative assignment included an essay as well as a design log. The essay accompanying the creative piece allowed me to analyze my own creative work as well as Tolkien's, developing a deeper understanding of the link between mythology and adaptation. The design log was an opportunity to fully understand my own process of creation: from interest to the formation of an idea and every step that led to the completion of the work.

Although the design log can be tedious, because inspiration can happen at any time in any place outside of actually working on the assignment, it was motivating to write down these ideas by texting myself or making notes on a scrap of paper when they struck, instead of relying on memory. It was a great way to keep thoughts and ideas organized by including brainstorms and rough drafts that could be used for reference. It also provided the opportunity to look back and see where I procrastinated, which was not always great to see on paper, and what I could improve on within my creative and academic process.

As the course went on, my interest in Tolkien grew more and more, especially as we learned about the medieval works that influenced him. My appreciation for the depth of his mythology came from reading the various adaptations he wrote of his own texts, reading his views of mythology and language, and being able to actively participate by creating adaptations of my own. As the course was ending, my interest in Beren and Lúthien was apparent through the poem I wrote, the painting I made, and the papers that accompanied them, resulting in the desire to continue my work from this class. I promptly wrote my proposal to do my English honors thesis on Tolkien's Beren and Lúthien story, including a poetic adaptation of the story in Old English–style alliterative meter in modern English.

This course reunited me with creative and abstract thinking and inspired an honors thesis that has given me confidence to continue into my master's degree work and eventually get my PhD. I owe the future of my academic career to this course, for it reminded me why I became a university student: to expand my mind and explore my creative and academic potential, all while engaging with a community of students who value the same things.

RESEARCHING THE SHAWSHANK TRAIL

Fan Pilgrimage and Service Learning

Maura Grady, Richard J. "Robby" Roberson Jr., and Erika Gallion

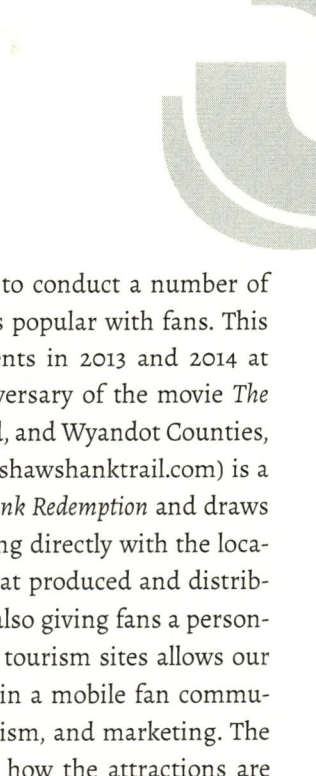

As teachers and researchers, we have teamed up to conduct a number of mixed-method studies of film tourism attractions popular with fans. This chapter discusses the work done with our students in 2013 and 2014 at Labor Day events celebrating the twentieth anniversary of the movie *The Shawshank Redemption* in Ohio's Ashland, Mansfield, and Wyandot Counties, located south of Cleveland. The Shawshank Trail (shawshanktrail.com) is a self-guided tour of filming sites from *The Shawshank Redemption* and draws fans seeking to connect with the film by interacting directly with the locations. The trail is not sponsored by the entities that produced and distributed the film, and, as such, it is sustainable while also giving fans a personalized, interactive experience. Studying local film tourism sites allows our students to be involved in their local region and in a mobile fan community as a way to learn about fandom studies, tourism, and marketing. The research activities—surveying fans to determine how the attractions are doing, in the fans' eyes—act as service learning projects. Through service learning, students can see how their studies apply to the real world and can realize positive effects on learning objectives such as demonstrated complexity of understanding, problem analysis, critical thinking, problem solving, and intellectual development. The students learn about data collection and gather information of value to local nonprofits.

According to Martin (2015), service learning is a pedagogical technique that combines academic learning with community service. Martin asserts that service learning "can provide a very valuable learning experience by taking classroom content and applying it in a real-life situation." The benefits are that "students use their classroom knowledge and skills [and] they also help community members in the process" (110). Placing students in situations where they need to communicate with diverse groups of people, make local contacts, and work with local businesses and organizations offers them the opportunity to develop improved interpersonal and professional skills while completing their course work.

In our case, we developed relationships with a number of local nonprofit organizations and small businesses that welcomed the students' help with a large-scale data collection survey on customer responses to the services these entities provided—in this case, the chance to visit filming locations for *The Shawshank Redemption*. The idea to build a *Shawshank* tourism attraction for fans to visit came originally from local fans of the film, Bill and April Mullen of Upper Sandusky, Ohio. Bill and April had been thrilled to have Hollywood set up shop in their own community and became fans and collectors of *Shawshank* memorabilia after the 1993 filming in their town in Upper Sandusky, Ohio. They created a network of locals who had worked as extras and crew members and traveled to connect with many of the film's actors, striking up friendly acquaintances with Bob Gunton (Warden Norton) and Morgan Freeman (Red) at first and later with Mark Rolston (Boggs), William Sadler (Heywood), and Frank Medrano (Fat Ass). When the filming location for the film's prison woodshop scenes came on the real estate market, they purchased it and painstakingly tracked down the original woodworking equipment used in the film that had since been sold off. They called the building the Shawshank Woodshop and formed a nonprofit organization for the purpose of raising money for the restoration of the nearby Wyandot County Court House (used in the film for Andy's trial scenes). In 2008, at the fifteenth anniversary of the filming, they held a reunion at the Shawshank Woodshop for actors, extras, crew, and fans. They staged a reenactment of the beloved opera scene from the film and collected donations for the courthouse (Shawshank Redemption and Lady Justice). Then in 2011, the famous oak tree from the film was sheared in half by high winds, and the story was reported by the national media, including NPR (Turner 2011). Soon fans began calling the Mansfield Convention and Visitors Bureau (CVB) asking whether they could visit the tree and other filming locations. After that, according to Mansfield CVB Group Tour and Media Director Jodie Snavely, the phone kept ringing at the CVB office, and it was determined that fans might want a map to guide them in visiting the filming locations.

Eventually, in collaboration with the Mullens, the Mansfield Reformatory Preservation Society (MRPS), the Ashland CVB, and other stakeholders, the Shawshank Trail was formalized as a tourist attraction, complete with a website, maps, podcasts, and themed merchandise. When we began working with the trail in 2013, plans were underway for the twentieth anniversary filming reunion, which would celebrate this beloved film, invite those involved in the production to reminisce, and present the Shawshank Trail to fans from all over the world.

The trail personnel wanted to know what fans might like to experience during the event, and we suggested opportunities for interaction with other fans, with those involved in the production, and with the locations themselves. As nonprofit groups, the Shawshank Woodshop, MRPS, and the CVBs had very limited funds for market research, so we and our students provided a valuable resource in the collected data. The 2013 survey questions (appendix B) focused on demographics, media awareness, and the factors of importance and satisfaction. The data suggested improvements for a similar event in 2014, when a new survey was conducted.

The student data collectors were enrolled in one of two courses: (1) an interdisciplinary honors course focused on local Ohio history and geography (2013), and (2) a market research class (2014). The work at times went beyond data collection as the students reflected on their own sense of themselves as fans of popular culture, their observations about the *Shawshank* fans' experiences at the film tourism attractions, and their understanding of the importance of improving communication among fans, scholars, and the nonprofit groups.

The timing of the first survey, Labor Day 2013, meant that we had only a brief period in which to orient students to their task (classes began two weeks before the survey). The honors program interdisciplinary seminar is "devoted to various topics related to the Honors Program mission of challenging the mind and participating in an intellectual community devoted to discussion and dialogue" ("Honors Program Current Courses" 2016). Faculty in different disciplines teach the course in two to four segments of several weeks each. The 2013 course theme was "Local/Ohio" with "*Shawshank Redemption*, Fan Culture, and Film Tourism in Ohio" as the first unit (four weeks). The sixteen students represented a variety of majors in the colleges of arts and sciences, business, education, and nursing and health sciences, but they had the following in common: (1) a level of engagement with materials perhaps more advanced than the average undergraduate at our institution in their junior or senior year, and (2) the fact that most students were veterans of several seminarlike courses that required inquiry-driven research writing. The interdisciplinary nature of the course required students to switch modes fairly smoothly and to work in disciplines outside their usual areas of competence, and the course itself required reflective writing to accompany the research project.

STUDENTS AND FANDOM STUDIES

Erika Gallion, a student in the 2013 course, has provided us with the following reflections:

> Fan culture is often dismissed by academics as a silly and amateur hobby. Dr. Maura Grady initiated the course by delivering reading material that suggested a different view of fan culture. What if fan culture elevated a film or a television show? What if fan culture provided more than these films or television shows could provide independently? These questions began to make sense in my mind as I envisioned my own participation in certain kinds of fandom. Didn't I believe that being a fan of *Harry Potter* or *Game of Thrones* meant going further than simply reading the books and watching the films or television episodes? I was part of these fan cultures because I participated in learning about and sharing the subjects after the films ended. I had blogged about certain episodes or book chapters, leading to interactions with other members of fan culture. Tumblr bridged the distance from me to other fans, allowing for discussions and friendships to blossom via the Internet. Because of a shared passion for a particular subject, friendships were formed. This, I realized, was fan culture: having a deep interest in something, sharing that passion with other fans, and partaking in discussions and events that allow this passion to grow.

In addition to learning about the discipline of fan studies, the students were required to engage in a crash course on *The Shawshank Redemption* and what tourism researchers call film-induced tourism (i.e., visiting filming locations in person). On the first day of class, students received an explanation of the unit along with a schedule of readings, assignments, discussions, and off-campus events (appendix B). Rather than start with the list of survey questions, students began the unit thinking about the following guiding questions:

> What is a fan?
> How do fans behave?
> Do fans *have* to participate in communal activities?
> Who are the fans of *Shawshank*?
> Why do fans want to visit filming locations?

What are fans looking for when they get there?
What is unique about the fans of *Shawshank* and/or Stephen King?

We consulted the organizers of the Shawshank Trail to choose questions for the survey, and we also checked out recent scholarship in fan studies and in tourism research. We looked to ascertain whether the responses of visitors to the trail bore out the assumptions of the two scholarly disciplines. We also looked to capture key demographic data for the trail to improve understanding of the fans and their desires so that the fans' needs could be better served in the future.

In the first week of the course, students prepared for the survey by viewing the film *The Shawshank Redemption* (Darabont 1994) and studying the Shawshank Trail's website. They also began reading and discussing several texts on fan studies and tourism research, the first of which was the preface from Hills's *Fan Cultures* (2002). The students needed to engage in some of the central questions of fan studies before they began surveying fans. Very quickly the students gained a shared vocabulary for examining fan cultures, began formulating their own definitions of fandom, and placing themselves as fans and fan scholars. In an online discussion, one student, an actuarial science major, said the following about Hills's text:

> Matt Hills sure can cover his tracks! In an amusing excerpt Hills tackles the difficult definition of fan culture by first attacking and providing issues with some of the most well accepted methods in this struggle for identification. He even goes as far as to discredit himself and mention many of his surefire contradictions he will create, maybe in a manner that can ultimately open the mind of the reader and destroy all preconceptions.... Too often we search for closure and surefire conclusions to issues that cannot be so quickly controlled. Fandom is certainly one of those subjects.

The students quickly grasped the idea that studying fans would be contradictory and complex. The students hypothesized what they might learn from interacting with and observing fans during the 2013 reunion weekend. Another actuarial science student responded to Hills by speculating how the upcoming survey at a fan event would play out: "I can guess that fans would be looking for sites and stories and memorabilia that would make the movie more real to them. They are probably looking for the kind of excitement that naturally accompanies learning more about something of which one is fond.

From looking at the exhibits and programs available, I think that fans will definitely find what thay [sic] are looking for when they visit."

Students then read an example of an ethnographic profile of a fan community in Mikhaylova (2012) and toured the Ohio State Reformatory, the iconic former prison used as the primary location in the film. The goal of the tour was to help students understand what visiting fans would be experiencing and to gain some knowledge of the building and the history of the filming to share with fans. A psychology major wrote the following on our post-tour discussion thread:

> I really enjoyed the tour of the [reformatory]. It was really exciting to see the places that were in the movie, and also fascinating to learn about the real history of the prison. The most interesting thing to me was probably seeing all of "Andy's" books just sitting there in storage and finally being taken care of after all these years. I had never before thought about what they might have done with the books after the movie, and learning that they were just sitting in a random room in the prison was fascinating. ... I think completing the tour made me appreciate the movie a lot more than I did before. There is just something exciting about being able to watch it on television and say "I've been there!" I think it makes the movie more real for me.

This student experienced what the organizers of the trail hope all fans will feel: the excitement of being able to interact *directly* with the film they love.

For the survey, we arranged for the students to work in pairs at locations and times that were convenient. With events going on in three counties, the students had plenty of options to choose from, and we had ample coverage. We taught the students about respecting the personal privacy of the survey participants and how to elicit responses without leading questions, explaining that guiding the fans' answers could affect reliability by steering respondents to a predetermined outcome. The 2013 students were given Shawshank Trail Staff buttons or lanyards, clipboards, maps, and additional event schedules to hand out if the fans needed them. Their knowledge of the film and locations enabled them to answer questions to help the fans feel at ease during the event.

After establishing a frame of reference for the film, we next prepared the students as market researchers. Using the actual data-gathering instrument as an example, the students were taught about the relevant marketing concepts. The students identified which interesting demographic data might come from their research. The research project required that the students learn about the appropriateness of both qualitative and quantitative information and when each type of data could be useful. After this theoretical groundwork had been laid, we then used the same survey instrument to illustrate the limitations of data gathering in the real world. The necessity to gather as much information as possible, as easily and as quickly as possible, with limited resources presented an interesting balancing act. The students quickly became aware of the challenges represented by concepts such as response rate, open-ended vs. closed-ended questions, relevance, reliability, and validity.

The issues of consent and privacy were also of utmost importance. We trained the students in accordance with policies from the institutional review board (IRB) for the university. Approval of the research design from the IRB was necessary before any research was undertaken. With the assurance that no subject was likely to be harmed, the next step was to familiarize the students with the concerns of consent. The instructor, working in conjunction with the IRB, created a script (appendix B) for the students to use when approaching prospective participants to inform them of who they were, of the purpose of the study, and of the ability to not participate, as well as to gather contact information for the researcher. The students were required to use this script whenever approaching an interview subject. The IRB guidelines were new to the students, for the most part, and the students were curious to understand why the guidelines were necessary, asking, "Why do we have to do all this just to talk to someone?" The survey was thus a good opportunity to teach students about the process of human research and to examine the question of what is ethical. For fan studies, this is a big question: How are fan scholars to conduct ethical research on fans? Our work showed students that there are established ethical procedures in place when human beings are used as data points, and this also allowed them to see the gray area in real life.

We spent considerable time training the students to be data gatherers. The students, after being taught the underlying concepts and being trained in appropriate behavior regarding human subjects, were then trained in use of the survey instrument. We conducted role-playing and mock interviews to make the students comfortable and familiar with the process of data gathering and interacting with the subjects. The students also rehearsed the consent statement. The 2014 students were also trained on the use of mobile device applications that were used to gather the data.[1]

The students collected 226 usable responses to the survey in 2013 and 111 in 2014. The 2013 data eventually yielded a number of significant results, including correlations between merchandise satisfaction and return intention (Roberson and Grady 2015). Based on our analysis of the 2013 data, we recommended a number of suggested improvements to the Shawshank Trail organizers, including increased merchandising, use of social media, and online media penetration, which would help secure sustainability for the trail beyond these special events. By building lasting relationships among fans, the local community, and the nonprofit organizations, the locations can remain accessible and can even enhance their offerings as they earn enough to maintain and renovate the historical buildings.

MARKETING AND FAN STUDIES

Erika's reflections on the connections between the local area and the university follow:

> The Shawshank Redemption has deep connections to [the area] where Ashland University . . . is located. An ideal location prompted Dr. Grady to assign students to participate in a very special experience: The Shawshank Trail's reunion of fans, extras, and crew. This reunion [was] designed to show fans the locations of where The Shawshank Redemption was filmed. The reunion encouraged fans from all over the world to tour . . . recognizable locations from the film such as the park bench Brooks fed birds on and the tree where Andy hid a note for Red. The Trail [event] also permitted fans to meet Bob Gunton, the actor who portrayed Warden Norton in the film. Having this event, I believe, helps The Shawshank Redemption live on: fans come together, providing their own perspectives on the film, allowing for continuous fresh takes on the film.

For the follow-up survey in 2014, marketing students served as data collectors. They were members of a section of Principles of Marketing, a sophomore-level course in the College of Business at Ashland University and a requirement for all majors (hospitality, fashion merchandising, marketing, business administration) in the college. The course required the twenty-five students enrolled to participate in a market research project, which that term took the form of surveying fans at the reformatory during the celebration of the twentieth anniversary of the release of The Shawshank Redemption. This event allowed students to conduct actual market research to glean insights about the attendees at the festivities; the *emphasis* for this group of students differed significantly, although the actual work was similar. As part of the preparation for the event we taught the marketing students about the content and impact of the movie and gave them a guided tour of the facility where filming occurred.[2] This familiarization and education was part of the training for conducting market research so that the students would be familiar with the context of the data they would be gathering.

The marketing students differed from our first group, the honors interdisciplinary seminar students, in a significant way: the marketing students' course objectives gave no consideration to questioning the value and intentions of studying fans; the marketing students saw fans as a target market for a product. The honors interdisciplinary seminar's scope required students to question the very premise of the study and of the scholarship on fandom, something not within the scope of the marketing course.

The honors students were most interested in what the fans had to say and how what fans said aligned with the assumptions students had formed from the preparatory materials and discussions. The marketing students were most interested in accurately collecting what the fans said. Although it's a bit of an oversimplification, we might say that the honors students were interested in content, but the marketing students were interested in data: asking questions such as "Did I follow the format correctly?" and "Was the survey valid?" It was the same activity but with a different emphasis, given the specific disciplinary orientation of each group of students.

After the completion of the event, we required the students to complete assignments about market research. A two-pronged approach was used. The first required the students to compile and interpret the information they gathered and to speculate on what larger trends might emerge when all the data were examined. The second part required the students to examine the design and justify improvements to the data-gathering instrument.

In evaluating the postsurvey discussions with both groups, we were struck by the difference in the student experiences of a similar task. The honors students, though also trained in IRB and proper survey techniques, were still most interested in the content of the fans' responses to the survey. They had formulated hypotheses ahead of time on what fan responses might be and what picture might be formed of the "typical Shawshank fan," even as they understood how problematic the formulation of such a picture might be. Their reflections included storytelling, an analysis of the nature of survey taking, and an evaluation of the roles they themselves played as agents in the study.

A history and political science major stated the following: "When collecting data at the Ohio State Reformatory . . . I met a husband and a wife in their mid-fifties who worked on the set of the film. Most of the movie was filmed in Mansfield, Ohio, so many locals were extras in the movie or on the set. This particular couple was eager to talk about their experiences, and, because I had to wait for at least another thirty minutes before I could start taking surveys, I was eager to listen." The couple had been involved in building the rock wall for the powerful sequence in which Red finds the treasure box Andy left underneath the iconic Oak Tree.

Although this student spoke with dozens of fans that day, this exchange stood out in his mind as he summarized his experience of the unit:

> The movie, according to the couple, was "a community event." In a way, the whole town got behind the movie. Perhaps that is one of the reasons The Shawshank Trail's 20 Year Reunion was so successful. While people from all over the country came to Mansfield, Ohio to see the sites, many locals came out of the woodwork to reminisce about their time on the set of *The Shawshank Redemption*. To many people all across the world, the film and its message have a sentimental value, but to the people of Mansfield, it seems, the movie is something more: it is a piece of them.

We did not ask the marketing students to reflect on their experience in ways similar to the honors students; instead, their focus was on the proper collection of accurate and usable data for the "client," the Shawshank Trail. The students may have had thoughts about the fans they spoke to, but the context of the course did not ask for their reflections, and the students' focus was instead on accurate data collection techniques.

Nonetheless, although the marketing students may not have reflected on the experience in the same way as the honors students did, there is still great value in this research for them and for fandom studies. Many students at the beginning of their college career have a limited view of the types of businesses that exist in their area or of the possibilities for themselves as workers or entrepreneurs. By engaging in this research for the Shawshank Trail, students can see that there are small businesses and nonprofit organizations formed as the result of demands by a niche market (in this case, a fan community) that demands respect and attention. The Shawshank Trail is not the work of the original artists: Stephen King, Frank Darabont, Castle Rock Entertainment, and Warner Brothers had nothing to do with its creation or its current operation. Instead the trail was born in response to fan demand and enthusiasm.

In addition, the project shows students the messy side of market research. The organizers of the Shawshank Trail needed to know who their market was in order to serve it well. In this kind of project, the students learn to deal with something that may not be a clearly defined product, and therefore they listen *better* in order to serve their market's needs. Having the students actually perform market research lets them learn by doing. By looking at the answers to the survey, they can learn that they have been asking some of the wrong questions and thus discover that the process they thought would be fairly straightforward is actually complex and messy.

CONCLUSION

Erika's reflection on the answers found to the guiding course questions:

> Before taking Dr. Maura Grady's Fan Culture course, I had never before studied film, let alone a culture based around fandoms. Reading the course description prompted an obvious question: what is Fan Culture? During the course, this question would be answered not once, but multiple times in a variety of ways.

The students' dedicated work in 2013 and 2014 not only exposed them to fans in action through direct participation in a large fan event, it also had them consider some of the challenges inherent in this interdisciplinary approach to studying fan tourists. The students' work yielded results that have already benefitted the Shawshank Trail: we were able to show the trail's organizers, for example, that fans who travel from farther away value fan-to-fan interaction more than local fans do, that fans valued the interaction with participants (actors, crew, and extras) more highly when they had traveled farther, and that fans who were not satisfied with the merchandise selection said they were less likely to return another time.

We also discovered that most visitors in 2013 wanted more interactive experiences and that they had heard about the event through traditional media (TV, newspaper, radio). These results can help the nonprofit groups target their advertising more effectively so that they reach fans outside the local area through a stronger online presence. In 2014 the Shawshank Trail did this very well with an increased Facebook presence and public relations that garnered stories on *Yahoo* and in the *New York Times*, the *LA Times*, the *Pittsburgh Post-Gazette*, and other outlets with an online presence. In 2014 the student data collectors' results showed that visiting fans were very satisfied with their experience, indicating that the changes, adjustments, and planning considerations influenced by the fan studies literature had yielded positive results. For the students, seeing their class work and fieldwork yield real benefits—not just for fans but also for the preservation of their community's important historical landmarks—was a positive experience. Through our students, we have been able to show local businesses and municipalities the importance of studying fans in a respectful manner. When fans are happy with the film tourism experience, they want to return, and many groups benefit, including the following:

1. The fans, who are able to visit preserved filming locations. Without the income generated by visitors, the Ohio State Reformatory would have been closed to the public long ago. Instead, it is able to restore and maintain the building for future visitors and is even expanding its role in historic preservation as the Official State Corrections Museum (Dech 2015).
2. The community, which sees an increase in the number of visitors to the area.
3. Local businesses, hotels, restaurants, and shops, which cater to visiting fans through specialized products and offers.

Fans may understandably be wary of participating in quantitative studies, but when the film tourism location is relatively new at providing services to fans and lacks external financial support (such as from the studio or major corporations), this kind of research is essential to preserving and improving the fan tourism experience, and students from all disciplines can learn valuable skills while also seeing that their work has real-world benefits beyond the classroom.

NOTES FOR CHAPTER 3

1. The use of mobile applications was adopted after the August 2013 survey, which was conducted by hand, and was tested in a November 2013 survey of another film tourism location (the Christmas Story House in Cleveland). The mobile apps allowed students to record the qualitative responses of survey participants as well as their quantitative responses, leading to easier data compilation.

2. Unlike the honors students, the marketing students did not examine the film and novella as a class, but several took it upon themselves to view the film on their own.

REBLOG, LIKE, AND FREEWRITE

Online Blogging Spaces in the Composition Classroom

Leslie Leonard and Lee Hibbard

Online spaces are dynamic; they adapt to accommodate the affinity groups that engage within them. We, as teachers and scholars, enjoyed these spaces long before we became teachers—as fans, as mutual followers, and as lovers of various media. Tumblr in particular afforded us a means to expand our identities as fans while engaging with a community of similarly invested users in discussions, questions, and lengthy explanatory text posts. On Tumblr we were able to construct an online identity that coincided with our interests rather than the usual social media identities found on Facebook or Twitter, which are tied to one's name or friends and family and are, as a result, excessively public and exposed. Rather, Tumblr's relative anonymity and the fact that it is a space geared toward users' interests made it the perfect online space in which to explore extracurricular activities in an interactive and community-centered way.

Lee came to Tumblr in 2014 and immediately made it a hybrid space for his popular culture interests—video games, in particular—and his academic life. For Lee, Tumblr was a place to reblog video game plays, gif files, and humorous text posts, but more important, it was a space in which to combine academia and fandom culture; it was hardly unusual to find him generating paper-length analyses or academic discussions with other users about the role of the uncanny in *Silent Hill*, of gender in *Mad Max*, or of the heroic tropes of comic book film adaptations.

Leslie likewise joined the Tumblr community in 2014, but she used the space initially for extracurricular interests. She primarily followed users who focused on generating superhero or comic book content, but as she began to follow more varied blogs she was drawn to the ongoing conversations that Tumblr posts created. Users were not just interacting with one another in what one might consider stereotypically fannish ways ("OMG I know! I love that book too!"); instead, users were engaging with the canonical media in creative ways and generating argumentative discussions with sources and in-depth analysis of scenes, writer motivation, and rhetorical strategies. As we developed further as scholars and instructors we began to see Tumblr's affordances as useful in an existing academia rather than merely as a place to merge our own interests with scholarly critique.

When we began teaching freshman composition classes, we found students who considered academic writing foreign, complicated, and unfamiliar; as a result, they often struggled in approaching the formal, graded writing that our classes required of them. As longtime participants of Tumblr, a website built for lengthy text posts and interactive, communal responses, we decided to merge the informal, social media writing that our students were already engaging in regularly and the high stakes, in-class writing that so often gave them pause.

These students were creative, intelligent, engaging, and, more important, loquacious in class and in their less-than-sneaky social media usage underneath desks or in separately opened desktop tabs. Why then did a freshly opened document disarm them so much? This problem, along with an interest in online writing practices, was the basis for our research. When not frozen at the prospect of a writing assignment, the students in our class texted, chatted, messaged, posted, retweeted, and reblogged with ease; they engaged easily in various online writing spaces, expressing opinions, creating narratives, and forming arguments, yet they considered this extracurricular writing entirely separate from higher-stakes academic writing. If, in fact, our students knew what they wanted to say, but felt intimidated and out of their depth in their academic writing, then perhaps we might use online writing to engage them in low-stakes activities that would make them comfortable with their own writing voices and their ability to craft and sustain an argument.

As Black (2010) emphasizes, online spaces such as Tumblr are inherently collaborative and require ongoing community interaction. Fan interaction on Tumblr often goes like this: A user somewhere around the world will post a question ("Why do people still consider this character a villain?"), an assertion ("OK, guys, but Parseltongue is really interesting from a linguistics point of view"), a public service announcement ("if a fic writer doesn't ask for constructive criticism, don't leave it"). Other users will reblog the original post with answers, questions, additions, edits, support, or disagreement, and thus an ongoing conversation is begun ("OMG, but have you thought about . . ."; "I disagree. I think the major issue here is . . ."; "Well, this scene shows that it's because . . ."). The discussions that take place are informal, multimodal, and often written to emphasize the particular writing voice of each user. If we could incorporate such informal written community participation into our classrooms, we hoped, our students would be able to engage with their peers in a social media format that many were already comfortable with, while also developing their writing voices and improving their traditional literacy skills (e.g., reading, writing, grammar, syntax). Our work demonstrates that by emulating the fan interactions that occur on Tumblr, students become more comfortable with their writing, they develop more honest critiques of their peers' work, and they begin to see academic writing as a far less daunting task than they did previously.

We taught two sections of English 101 and its studio component, respectively. Our students were college freshmen, typically English as a Second Language (ESL) students, many of whom required supplementary writing instruction, which they received outside regular class time in studio. Whereas many freshmen are required to take the English 101 course, which meets twice a week, some—typically ESL students or students entering college underprepared for collegiate writing—are also required to meet in a smaller studio class dedicated to giving the students supplemental instruction as well as writing time with an instructor present. These students meet with their studio section twice a week in addition to attending the English 101 section twice a week; this gives them four whole days of writing instruction. Our students completed the majority of their written work in studio, where class size is under twenty students, the students can more easily engage with their peers, and where they receive more personal teacher assistance.

Leslie's own initial work, in the fall semester of 2014, involved integrating online peer-review strategies into classroom lessons; through postreview interviews with the students, Leslie found that students not only desire criticism to become better writers, they are also more willing to give and receive honest criticism when involved in online-negotiated peer-review sessions. The two of us, both graduate teaching assistants at the University of Alabama in Huntsville, furthered this preliminary research in the spring semester of 2015. Both of us being familiar users of social media, we engaged two classes with the popular online blogging space of Tumblr as a base for student writing, reader responses, and final assessment portfolios.

Tumblr offers the affordances of sharing text posts, pictures, and videos with a large group of followers. Although Tumblr is typically used for individual blogging, this online community atmosphere helped our student writers develop through peer-to-peer learning. This chapter offers a description of our classroom practice as well as our findings from pre- and post-semester surveys and student interviews. By assessing students' experiences, we sought to understand the pedagogical gains of engaging Tumblr from students, both those familiar with the recreational use of online fandom spaces and those encountering them for the first time. We found that even though initial student involvement with Tumblr was low, these students were optimistic about their ability to learn the site and later found it to be useful in the development of their writing processes. The students felt more engaged with the academic writing we asked of them once we implemented daily, informal, low-stakes writing on an interactive blog.

Throughout this research we employ terms such as *online blogging, online writing, fandom spaces,* and *fan-based blogs* in reference to diverse new media practices. To avert misunderstanding we would like to use this space to define these terms and our use of them more precisely. When we note that students are constantly and actively engaged in online blogging and online writing outside the classroom, this encompasses any type of blogging or writing the students may be active in including on Facebook, Twitter, Tumblr, Blogspot, Wordpress, Reddit, and YouTube commentary. However, the online writing and blogging our research specifically investigates is community blogs, fandom spaces, and online writing, specifically that of Tumblr. The difference between fandom spaces and other social media communities, in our work, is that these fandom-based activities involve an active community of people passionate about a similar theme or work and who are constantly engaging with that work and connecting with others in an online platform through art, comments, feedback, writing, edits, and revisions, all in a communal space. Our hope is that when we use the terms *fandom* or *fan-based* it brings to mind this specific community-centered gathering of people engaged with one another for a similar purpose. That is a central point of our findings.

Although Henry Jenkins and others acknowledge that online blogging and writing spaces have long been part of students' lives outside the classroom, we have found in our own classrooms that many students do not interact with online writing spaces as often as other social sites. However, by incorporating these sites, we can create a mode of teaching writing that complements the skills of those students familiar with online spaces and introduces others to a new and intuitive means of developing their ideas. By using these sites in the composition classroom, teachers can update their assignments and assessments to work in conjunction with the new media to better engage and respond to students.

As new media infiltrate traditional modes of composing in the classroom, teachers must incorporate new ways of assigning and assessing writing as well. In certain online communities, which Curwood, Magnifico, and Lammers (2013) label "fan-based affinity spaces," students are actively and creatively writing toward a specific purpose and audience while conducting community-centered peer review on their own terms to further develop themselves as writers; as new media scholars define them, "these spaces often spread across many sites, including... message boards, blogs," and fan fiction publishing sites (678). The fan fiction and blog prompts being written in these spaces are perhaps, at first glance, very different from the expository and print-based essays typically asked of students; however, upon looking closer at the strategies incorporated in this "affinity space" writing, one can see how the two—academic writing and creative online composition—might draw on each other to create a more effective means of teaching writing in the modern age (677).

LITERATURE REVIEW

Online blogging and writing spaces have long been part of students' lives outside the classroom. Even students unfamiliar with fandom-based forums actively engage with informal online spaces such as Facebook, Twitter, and Instagram. Despite the differences in academic and online writing, many recent fan study scholars, such as Rebecca Black and Karen Hellekson, have found that student writing is improved by certain skills developed in these online communities. Despite the fact that many students struggle with writing in a classroom setting, the same students are able to write, respond, and receive criticism easily within an online sphere.

If we look more specifically at the practices of online fan-based blogging spaces and the writing students produce there, it is easy to notice that student writers, when not being timed, graded, or pushed to use pencil and paper, naturally utilize effective composition skills that can be brought back to the classroom to create more productive writing (Hellekson and Busse 2006). Bloggers and users of social media sites such as Tumblr compose lengthy, articulate, and often academically minded posts devoid of classroom prompting and simultaneously respond to, edit, and critique the work of their online peers—all within a close community wherein each user is at any given moment a writer, a reader, a responder, an editor, and a critic. It is again worth emphasizing that these users create content and respond to others' work spontaneously and unprompted, which demonstrates the organic communicative nature of such social sites as well as offers a model for more organic and effective classroom write-read-respond exercises.

Some sources coined the term *affinity spaces* for these online fan-centric forums, whereas others have labeled them *participatory cultures*, a term that emphasizes the "low barriers" of these spaces (Curwood et al. 2013, 1) and the strong support for "artistic expression" (Jenkins 2006b, 3). Despite whatever term scholars prefer, however, all discern the collaborative work being done in these spaces (Jenkins 2006b; Black 2009). Each of these scholars' works are primarily based in fan studies. Scholars such as Black study the effects of fan fiction on traditional writing, whereas Jenkins is particularly interested in online community interaction. In all cases, each scholar notes that the primary function of such online spaces, particularly for fans, is to serve as a space for collaborative work and conversation about a theme or an existing work. As several sources acknowledge, these sites are "social communities" formed by "common endeavors" and "participation" (Jenkins 2006b, 9); however, there is more to these spaces' emphasis on community beyond the fact that they must be dynamic to continue (Burns and Webber, 2009).

According to Hellekson and Busse (2006), these sites and the posts and the works produced there depend largely on "community-centered creation," involving "constant manipulation, renegotiation, commenting, and revising" (6). With this community-centered aspect in mind, online communities incorporate their own self-driven peer-review and work-in-progress collaboration while integrating advanced composition skills independent of any classroom setting (6). Hellekson and Busse were deeply entrenched within various fan spaces long before they began their scholarly work on the subject, and both maintained active profiles as writers and readers of fan fiction on sites like Livejournal. Their prior experience in the fan fiction community is imperative to note: we recommend it for any instructors or scholars interested in the abilities of these communities.

Tracey Kell (2009), a high school English teacher, conducted a fan fiction specific study of online practices that, as a result of the online site used, was less successful than intended; despite this, her study still provides a positive model for online feedback. Kell's class included fan fiction assignments in which her high school literature students posted their work in an online space and edited and reviewed one another's work online as well. Unfortunately, because the lessons were going to be incorporated into a high school classroom, which is far more regulated and structured by outside policies than a college class, she was unable to use a true online blogging site and instead was forced to create a space within the class for her students to write and engage in peer review—not unlike Google Drive, which, though useful, is far from any social media platform. An actual fan fiction site would have provided a fully developed community of writers, editors, and readers dedicated to engaging with existing works as well as a sophisticated tagging system, a myriad of genres, tropes, alternate universe fictions, and fandoms to choose from, and a specific mechanism for review and feedback that facilitates discussion in an organic and seamless conversation thread.

As a result, Kell (2009) admitted, the limitations of the school's Internet and its restricted sites resulted in the assignment not being "as fluid or fulfilling as it would have been on an official blogging site" (34). In this way Kell's study was not as successful as it could have been, because her students were unable to connect on an actual online site built for community interaction. Nevertheless, Kell's students were able to review and respond to one another's work in a similar online fashion. Relevant to our own work is that Kell found her students to be much more "honest in their review" in the limited "electronic peer feedback" that was conducted than in face-to-face peer review (32–33). Whereas face-to-face critique most often produces criticism that is subdued, overpolite, and ultimately unhelpful, what Kell's study shows (and what our own research corroborates) is that online review allows students a space to be more forthright (and therefore more constructive) in their criticism.

Kell (2009) demonstrates that the feedback, criticism, and editing skills used in online spaces, even when incorporated only minimally, can yield honest and effective student criticism. Most interesting is that Kell's classroom experiment led her to wonder whether teachers risk "undermining students' pop culture" by making it "institutionalized" within a classroom (34). Other scholars are also interested in this problem of co-opting student culture into the classroom; however, what is being proposed here is not that social media sites such as Twitter or Facebook be used to teach daily grammar and writing lessons, but rather that blogging sites such as Tumblr can provide interactive platforms for students to share and respond to informal writing. But what is most important, whether or not specific online sites are used for assignments, is that teachers can take the skills used independently on these sites and further develop them in the classroom; in some cases the actual sites themselves are irrelevant to the processes that can be gleaned from their example.

Each scholar mentioned previously touches briefly on the peer-to-peer aspect of these spaces and the beta editing and feedback stage of fan fiction creation, yet few expand on the importance of these interactions (Jenkins 2006b; Burns and Webber 2009). Hellekson and Busse (2006) describe the process of online composition as intrinsically linked to its "community-centered creation" (6). According to them, online writing necessitates "constant manipulation, renegotiation, commenting and revising, all done electronically among a group of people . . . intimately involved" in its creation. In this process, "the author . . . is a collective entity," and the pieces being produced in these spaces have a "dense intertextuality," which also ensures that they are never fully completed but rather are a continuous "work in progress" (6). As a result of this, authors depend heavily on their peers to review, edit, and provide a critique for rewriting. The idea that even published pieces—and, more important, the conversations about these pieces—are a never finalized work in progress is something that is stressed in academic writing classrooms, yet it occurs naturally in online discussions.

In order to further avoid the issue of co-opting student culture, we must emphasize that instructors should not choose popular social media sites or aspects of student culture purely for their application in the classroom; instead, teachers should be integrated into these social spaces and understand the existing community of those spaces before considering including them in instruction. It is acceptable for instructors to understand and be part of an online community and then adapt certain aspects of that for more developed and modern teaching, but it is important to ensure that the instructor's inclusion of social media does not devolve into simply pushing technology at students without a full understanding of how such social media operate. This chapter is not a guide for instructors to pick up at will, but rather an account of our own successes with an online platform that we were familiar with and saw the potentials of as a teaching tool.

METHODS

We designed our courses to take advantage of Tumblr affordances and use them to enhance student writing exercises. We chose to use Tumblr because both of us have been part of the Tumblr community for a while and because Tumblr does not have the word limitations of Twitter or the personal requirements of Facebook—even a closed Facebook group would sacrifice student anonymity. This is not to say that Tumblr offers more useful features for classroom teaching than other sites, only that it offers different features and that we were most comfortable using it since we were already integrated into the community. Teachers looking to use social media who are not familiar with Tumblr are encouraged to create low-stakes assignments from sites they are comfortable with, such as Twitter, Blogspot, and Facebook.

The important thing is that the teachers are part of these communities and are respectful and mindful of the culture within these spaces before using them for their own instructional practices. To illustrate this more fully, we can look at the ways in which fans use Tumblr as an affinity space: to share pictures, fan-made canon, and fiction and to communicate in a lexicon recognizable mainly to the specific fandom community and the Tumblr community at large. Various fan lexicons typically use abbreviations in place of full names when discussing various media within the community, so that a show like *How to Get Away with Murder* becomes "htgawm," and the film *Captain America: The Winter Soldier* becomes "catws"; these fandoms likewise create specific names or tags within communities that have little meaning to non–community members. Similarly, Tumblr employs a lexicon recognizable to users as they become more integrated into the site, so that "nsfw" is always adult content posts, "femslash" is always in reference to fictional female couples, and inspirational posts are tagged as "spo" (e.g., studyspo, fitspo, thinspo); each comes with a particular and cohesive community of its own.

In contrast to fan usage, student usage mostly entails communication outside Tumblr's various fan-based lexicons and does not participate in fandom exchange. It is important for instructors to understand the social media platform they wish to incorporate in terms of both the technical usage of the platform and the existing communities therein. However, because students are typically comfortable with online communication and informal Internet-speak, the fan-based blogging that they engage in on their own time, even something as innocuous as retweeting LeBron James, makes students generally well-suited to the informal writing asked of them through sites such as Tumblr even when they are not an explicit part of the Tumblr community.

Student familiarity with online writing on various social platforms means that they are well equipped for what Elbow (1997, 5) labels "low-stakes assignments," which prepare students for more rigorous, high-stakes academic writing. He adds that "the goal of low-stakes assignments is not so much to produce excellent pieces of writing as to get students to think, learn, and understand more of the course material." These assignments are ungraded and extremely informal, and as a result the students are able to explore their thoughts and become more comfortable in their writing before applying it to more academic, graded assignments.

Elbow (1997, 6) claims that for students, "writing *feels* like an inherently high-stakes activity" since students typically associate writing with school, "where it is virtually always evaluated, usually with a grade." However, modern students, even those not fully familiar with online spaces, use writing to communicate their ideas daily with texting, posting, tweeting, and a multitude of other informal writing outlets. What students lack, then, is the connection between this daily informal writing and its place in the commonly high-stakes class. Elbow helpfully explains that the more low-stakes writing students do, the more comfortable they become in their own writing voices and in their ability to more effectively introduce and explore their ideas.

When students' low-stakes writing is as communally participatory as online forums, it promotes the same natural peer review and intertextual conversations that these community-based sites demand. Teachers Paul Allison (2009) and Glen Bledsoe (2009), among others, focus on studying how students use online communities to further their low-stakes writing in the classroom. Much like our own work, Allison's research had students in a studio classroom "become members of a social network"—in this case Youth Voices, a school-based site centered on student writing. Allison's students developed blogs and connected with other student blogs and authors to form a network of writing and responding. As in our own classroom, Allison's students tagged their work to make it easy to find when searching the site, and they added their peers to a list of friends, making it easier "to follow each other's work in the future" (81). Allison's work pays particular attention to the way his students built intertextuality by constantly responding and interacting with one another's work. He notes that blogging was merely "the tool" that allowed him to better facilitate the community atmosphere and constant responses and reviews he desired in his classroom (90).

Like Allison, Bledsoe (2009) used online models to create a community of student writers in his fourth-grade class. The class composed a fictional narrative together, with each student being able to contribute and edit other students' ideas and additions to the story. In both studies the most important aspect of the online writing and publishing is the community that it necessitates.

Some of Tumblr's specific abilities and structures were particularly useful to the project of student-driven low-stakes writing. Tumblr users create a blog that comes complete with a username and icon picture, and they see content only from the users whom they follow. What this means, then, is that students must create a blog, invent a creative username, and find a picture to use as their icon; other students then recognize their peers' blogs by these icons and usernames. Because Tumblr allows students to post from behind a username and an anonymous icon picture, the instructor should always know which student is attached to which username, but the student's peers do not necessarily have to know which blog belongs to whom. Tumblr posts can also be made as formatted text posts, photos, videos, external links, or audio files; as a result of these options, students are able to make multimedia posts and responses.

Tumblr's main means of sharing information is through a blog's followers. Followers see everything a blog posts online and can respond to these posts; much like how Facebook posts can typically be seen only by "friends," Tumblr posts can be seen only by followers. It is important to note that because Tumblr organizes searchable hashtags, blogs that are not following your students can also see their posts if those posts have a popular hashtag. For instance, one of our students was a fan of Jimmy Kimmel, so if he had made a post talking about Jimmy Kimmel and tagged it as such (#jimmy kimmel), it would show up in the greater community under that tag and could be seen and responded to by users not in the class. If teachers wish to avoid this, they should simply have their students use only designated hashtags for their class, such as #daily freewrite, #EH101, or #peer review—or avoid tags altogether.

For our class we had the students create a personal blog on Tumblr, and if they already had a blog, then they made a separate one for the class. The students used anonymous usernames and followed their peers' blogs and the teacher's blog so that each person in the class could see the posted and reblogged content of everyone else. The students then did daily prompted freewrites and employed the hashtag system as a means of organizing their posts. Along with completing daily freewrites, in which the students employed informal language as well as videos, links, and images, the students also reblogged their classmates' posts and responded to them. In order to more effectively reblog their classmates' posts, the students typed the Tumblr username of the original poster into the hashtag section. Tumblr alerts the original poster that someone has responded to the blogpost so that this person can, in turn, respond directly to that blogger's additions to the post and build a conversation of responses based on the initial post topic.

Because Tumblr is a social media site that fosters an environment of community writing, we were especially interested in the success of ESL students, who could benefit from the peer-to-peer aspects of the site. More so than our native English-speaking students, our ESL students could benefit from the casual online writing, the community of peers to interact with online, and the fact that our inclusion of a blog meant constant daily public online writing in English. The student perspective accompanying this article is a collaborative work from two of our ESL students who found that their engagement with a community of their peers on Tumblr improved their confidence with peers in other classes and improved their skills as English speakers.

Because of Tumblr's multimodal posting capabilities, which allow students to include pictures, gifs, videos, text, audio, and links in any given post, our ESL students were able to post in various formats that allowed for expression beyond simply written text. This aided in their ability to communicate ideas in multiple formats while also allowing them to further connect the ideas that they were expressing in written English with visual or audio resources. Similarly, because the writing that typically takes place in online fandom spaces is informal, often abbreviated, and hyperbolic ("OMG! I love this chapter!"), ESL students were able to articulate ideas without the stress of academic, grammatically correct writing and without the fear of being immediately marked as a second-language learner by peers online (Black 2008b). Tumblr's varying, fandom-specific vocabulary likewise aided our ESL students, since Tumblr is a site that often requires users, especially those unfamiliar with particular hashtags or fandoms, to discern meaning from context. As a result, our ESL students gained practice and experience in determining the meaning of unfamiliar words or phrases through the multimodal context provided in a post.

Although most of our students had no previous interaction with Tumblr or blogging, they all quickly took to the informal and condensed style of the site. The site's condensed posts and easy commenting and reblogging ability, which makes the existing users' fan interactions on Tumblr so organic and community-based, similarly affected the writing of our students. We saw their daily freewrite exercises quickly become more informal, more succinct, and more engaged with what their classmates were writing. In postsurvey interviews the students listed freewriting assignments, the ability to comment on one another's posts, and the ability to read their peers' thoughts as helpful to their writing process. The students also admitted that writing about their essay topics beforehand helped them pinpoint which thoughts were most important faster, rather than taking paragraphs or pages, as they might have done in the essay without this previous online brainstorming.

We also facilitated student involvement on Tumblr by encouraging the students to access online resources on their personal devices such as smartphones, tablets, and laptops during class. Students typically keep these devices out during their classes and may even attempt to use them during class. Rather than oppose this, in our class we encouraged the students to keep these devices nearby and to engage them to complete assignments, freewrites, and lessons. The students used their phones, tablets, and other personal devices to blog, when prompted during class. This helped to keep them engaged and to associate the work that we were doing on Tumblr with their everyday social media usage.

Scholars like Allison (2009, 81) mention the affordances of online communities that allow students to easily interact with "peers who have similar interests and passions." On Tumblr these similar interests are accessed through the hashtag system that categorizes posts, so that when one of our students searched Tumblr for peers who were interested in Jimmy Kimmel, for instance, posts tagged as Jimmy Kimmel were the only results and made it easy for him to find blogs outside the class to follow and reblog. The tag system on Tumblr is typically used as an easy, search engine–like means of finding particular topics or communities.

For instance, users interested in aligning themselves with or reaching out to a community centered primarily on fitness inspiration would tag their posts as "fitspo" in order to ensure that their posts were visible to other users interested in the topic or active in the "fitspo" community. Likewise, many of our students used the hashtag system to find, follow, and align themselves with Tumblr fan communities outside the class blogs. So while some students used Tumblr only for the writing and responding that we did as a class, some searched Tumblr frequently for outside blogs and posts to bring into the discussion or simply to follow for their own fan-based enjoyment.

During a particular lesson on ethos, logos, and pathos in preparation for a rhetorical analysis essay, the students created their own examples or found outside examples of one or more of the rhetorical devices. After posting their examples, they reblogged other students' posts and commented on which kind of rhetorical device the student was demonstrating and why it was that device. Whereas before the lesson very few students had a clear grasp of the material, afterward nearly every student understood the function of the devices and how to determine their usage in a sentence or paragraph. The students noted that with Tumblr they could "check other people's thoughts" on the subject and that the assignment was "harder to understand without Tumblr." Unlike in a class discussion, in which not every student is willing to speak, each student participated; they found their own examples online in the media of their choice. Although in a class discussion it is difficult and time-consuming to check each student's comprehension, by having students post and reblog, we could easily monitor which students had a firm grasp on the material and which ones did not, simply by scrolling down our own blog's dashboard. This also presented an opportunity for peer-to-peer learning, since the students gave helpful tips for remembering and recognizing the appeals for their classmates.

Peer review on Tumblr was different from typical classroom peer review, not only because it was online and afforded relative anonymity but also because the students were not posting the entirety of their papers. Tumblr allows for lengthy text posts and has no character limit, but because Tumblr's layout displays each post stacked vertically down the screen, posting entire essays there would have required a lot of scrolling and would have made the peer review lengthy and not as effective. Instead, the students posted parts of their papers for review. For instance, they might post the introduction, the thesis, or the conclusion, and their peers would reblog and respond to those paragraphs or sentences. As a result, the students were able to receive more specific feedback on certain parts of their papers and could compare, for example, their own paper's thesis with those of their classmates and judge the strength of their intended argument. Many Tumblr users, particularly in the fan fiction community, already perform a similar method of community-based critique known as beta reading, which involves authors posting small preview portions of their stories or articles for other users in the community to read, edit, and provide feedback on. Similarly, the peer review that we conducted through Tumblr, because it was more focused on individual sections of student writing, provided more in-depth feedback on small sections of writing rather than general feedback on larger portions.

The students quickly became more comfortable responding to their peers, whether during peer review of their essays or during informal posts. Many of the students had never conducted peer review and had never run a blog before and so were particularly interested in receiving the responses and the feedback of their fellow students, which they said helped them brainstorm new ideas. A large part of what made commenting through Tumblr so much more effective than in-class peer review was the anonymity and informality that Tumblr afforded. Students commenting on one another's essays in a formal classroom setting and then returning those essays to the original author with their critiques often results in less-than-critical remarks that are unhelpful, most often written with the feelings of the author in mind rather than the effectiveness of the work. We found that when students responded online to one another, they were more willing to offer genuine feedback that was more critical and more helpful. Even when students knew the icons and usernames of their peers, the level of imagined anonymity that such usernames and icons afforded enabled the students to offer authentic opinions and lengthy reviews of their peers' work that they otherwise would not have offered if forced to confront their peers face-to-face. With online fan practices, it is well-known that the relative anonymity that online spaces provide users often results in a loss of inhibition in expressing straightforward comments and feedback; similarly, our students were able to create more honest responses as a result of such online anonymity. However, many online comment spaces can often change quickly from helpful feedback to unnecessary or hurtful criticism. Our classroom was free of such concerns, most likely as a result of the academic setting and the nature of the work that the students engaged in through Tumblr.

Students also used Tumblr to brainstorm topic ideas for papers, create essay outlines, share links to outside resources such as scholarly articles and online copies of class readings, and post sections of their own essays for their peers to reblog and review.

As we mentioned previously, the goal of low-stakes writing is to urge students to be more comfortable with both their writing and their own voices. As a result, the ungraded assignments our students completed regularly on Tumblr made them more confident in their ability to get to the point of what they had to say in their graded writing. Whenever students struggled with an idea, we would either return to Tumblr as a class and informally brainstorm solutions or we would have the student explain their idea to us as if they were online, describing it casually and concisely. The students became more comfortable with their own writing voices the more they wrote online.

The students' increased comfort with their writing voices and writing ability came as a direct result of Tumblr's fan-based platform. Much like the fan interactions that take place on Tumblr, our students' writing quickly became more succinct and more informal. Similarly, as a result of Tumblr's tagging system, which allows fan communities to search for and find one another, students often posted about self-chosen topics that interested them, whereas Tumblr's reblogging capabilities encouraged comments and feedback in an organic and conversational way.

Although Black (2010, 75) describes "traditional literacy skills, such as reading, writing, speaking, and listening" as "just starting points" for the media-bred literacy of the twenty-first century, our research aims to show that these new media-based skills can work in tandem to improve "traditional literacy skills" rather than considering them as separate categories. In her work with fan fiction, Black emphasizes that classrooms must change their expectations for student literacy to include emerging technologies and multimodal skills. In the academic future that Black imagines, students will be pressed to expand their literacy to include not only the traditional literacy skills that she outlines but also twenty-first-century literacies such as online communication, "synthesizing electronic information," and even "recognizing the complex ethical dimensions of online environments." Although our work agrees heavily with Black's assertion that student literacy must evolve alongside increasing technological advancements and the complexities of online culture, our own work, because it is deeply rooted in the specific academic requirements of freshman composition courses, is more interested in recognizing the advanced community-based writing, reading, and editing that takes place in online communities in order to apply it to what Black labels "traditional literacy skills." As a result, we hope to use the twenty-first century technological literacy available to online communities to supplement and aid traditional student literacy.

FINDINGS

We decided to conduct student surveys to gauge student interest, ability, and engagement in the use of social media in the first-year composition classroom. We conducted surveys among two studio classes to increase our sample size, since studios are designed with small teacher-to-student ratios in mind. These surveys functioned as a measurement of student self-assessment and gave us baseline data to correlate with our daily observation of classroom activity and interviews conducted with students to further investigate student involvement in social media and how this related to the writing classroom. By having both surveys as well as our own classroom

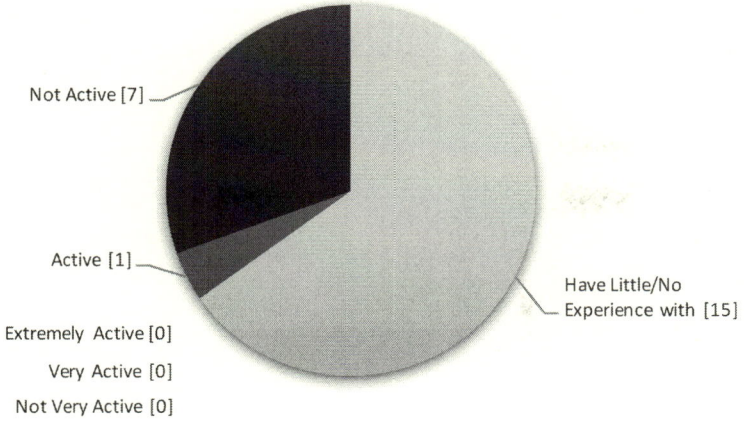

FIGURE 5 | Level of familiarity of students in the course with Tumblr, by numbers of responding students.

observations and student self-assessments, we could employ a sufficient amount of both statistical data and individual reflection to determine how students perceived the course and their involvement in social media activities. The goal of these findings is to empirically show student improvement and interest in writing classes paired with social media and as a result gauge the effectiveness of such classes.

In our initial survey we found that even though none of the students were wholly unfamiliar with sites such as Facebook, 63 percent of them had no knowledge of Tumblr before this course, and 38 percent of them had no knowledge of other online personal blogs at all. The pie chart featured here (fig. 5) shows the 63 percent of students who responded as having little or no knowledge of the site. Other percentages shown describe how active students considered themselves to be on social blogging sites, with the majority reported as being "Not Active."

Many of our students were ESL students and were far more familiar with online chat sites that they had used frequently in their home countries. These students' previous experience with chat sites proved relevant in their responses to reblogged posts, which quickly became informal and contained many attributes of casual online chatting. Likewise, although the majority of our students had no previous experience with online blogging, they were still familiar with Internet culture, texting, and other forms of social media. Their experience with other social media sites gave them a foundation in blogging terminology. For instance, terms such as *liking, posting, following,* and *tagging* were all familiar, and they easily picked up terms like *reblogging*.

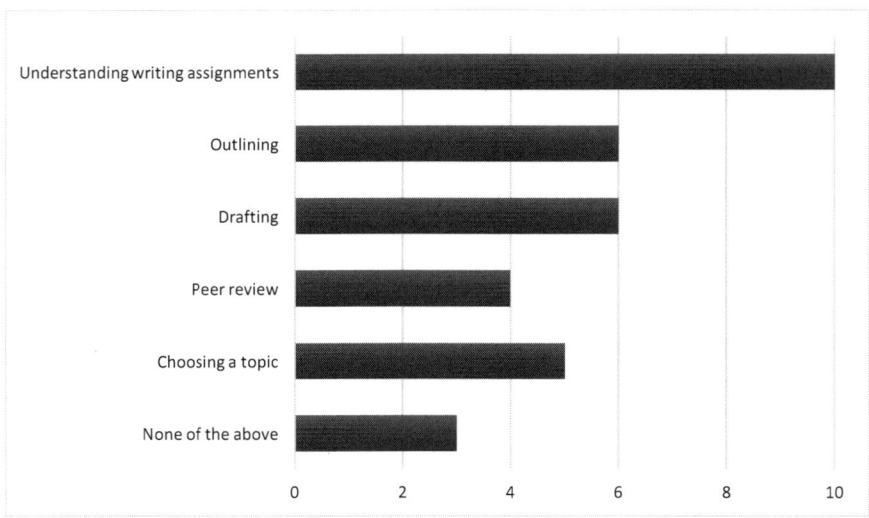

FIGURE 6 | Responses to the question "What part of the writing process has our class use of Tumblr helped most with" by numbers of students.

When we asked, "What part of the writing process has our class use of Tumblr helped most with?", 48 percent of the students noted that Tumblr specifically helped them to better understand the formal writing assignments; 29 percent considered Tumblr most helpful for both outlining and essay drafting; 24 percent believed that Tumblr improved their ability to develop a productive topic; and 19 percent thought Tumblr was most useful for peer review. Only 14 percent said that Tumblr was not helpful to their individual writing process. The students were able to choose more than one option, and the results are shown here (fig. 6).

Our use of Tumblr, 67 percent of the students admitted, made them more interested in class writing, including assigned formal essays. Our survey also showed that 81 percent of the students had a high interest in the writing in our class in particular, as opposed to in other classes or having little or no interest.

We found that even though the majority of our students had little or no prior knowledge of online blogs (63 percent, we have noted, had no prior knowledge of Tumblr at all), nearly all thought that the site would be easy to learn. During our postsurvey we saw that even students with no prior blogging knowledge found Tumblr to be easily accessible and intuitive for users.

ANALYSIS OF FINDINGS

Despite any time limitations in our research, with our findings above we conclude that Tumblr is not only an exceptional online platform for low-stakes writing assignments, it is also effective at garnering student interest and engagement within the first-year composition classroom. As Black (2008b, 406) writes in one of her many chapters on fan fiction's effects on ESL student writing, students are able to "write about topics of their own choosing" in a meaningful and informal way while engaging with peers in a social online setting that is familiar to them because of its easily navigable social media format. Scholars such as Rebecca Black, Karen Hellekson, and Henry Jenkins acknowledge that because these sites are built for fan interactions that are entirely community-driven, they lend themselves to participatory intercommunication. As a result, students find themselves writing frequently and voluntarily as part of a community of their peers with shared common interests that often extend beyond the class and its assignments.

Despite initial student involvement with Tumblr being low, the students later found it to be useful in the development of their writing process. Overall, the students felt more engaged with the academic writing we asked of them once we implemented daily, informal, low-stakes writing on Tumblr's interactive blog. Students also admitted to feeling more interested in the class as a whole and in the writing done in this class compared to the assignments of other classes.

In future classes, preferably in English 102 classes or in 101 classes that do not feature the studio section as a required supplement, we hope to have students engage more with Tumblr and other social media sites such as Twitter. We will push students in future classes to engage with the site more outside class time; the students will also follow published authors, blogs, and accounts besides merely those of their peers. In future classes we will have students interact more with the sites' capabilities: uploading videos, images, links, and full papers; searching tags for outside blogs and posts that might be relevant to an assignment; and incorporating these multimedia capabilities into the presentation of their formal essays.

Through our use of informal blogging, students were able to write freely, incorporate media into their writing, organize their ideas in a clear and concise manner, and become more comfortable and engaged with the class as a result. We were also able to respond to students in a more informal manner and assess their progress through more than simply their high-stakes, graded assignments. This has created a wealth of new material and teaching methods in our classroom, and we hope to continue and improve our research in future classes so that we might join student engagement on social media with traditional composition lessons in order to create further pedagogical developments. Furthermore, by encouraging students in future composition classes to engage online outside their lessons and build an online community made up of their classroom peers, we should expect to see these students involved and engaged more with their peers and their classes. This heightened student involvement in introductory composition courses could directly affect collegiate issues such as freshman retention rate. However, we can see more immediate results in the way students interact online and the way both students and teachers can informally communicate and build student low-stakes writing on various social media platforms.

We did not intend for our incorporation of Tumblr to be geared for ESL classrooms, yet many of our findings can be particularly useful for ESL students. Constantly typing posts and responses helps these students practice their English, particularly where grammar is concerned, and many of our ESL students especially benefited from messaging back and forth with native English-speaking students about class topics and assignments. Likewise, because many of the assignments involved writing online, which offers more time to express one's thoughts, students who would typically not add to classroom discussion because of their lack of English skills found an outlet wherein they felt comfortable offering feedback and communicating freely with their classmates.

As we stated before, this chapter is merely a detailing of our own successful experiences with social media in our classrooms, and we do not advocate that teachers who are not part of these online communities pick them up at will for their own teaching practices. Yet for teachers who *are* part of various online communities, the best means of incorporating most social media sites into the classroom is to keep them close to their original purpose. These sites are meant for informal social interaction and, as such, are perfect for low-stakes assignments. For the writing classroom, any assignment that gets students writing is a good place to start, whether that be through reaction posts (How do you feel about...), brainstorming exercises, opinion pieces, or other formats. Social sites are perfect platforms for peer-to-peer communication and shared information, so the assignments should emphasize student interactions and generate discussion, whether in the classroom or online.

USING TUMBLR IN THE CLASSROOM

Reflections on EH101S

Lingzi Yuan and Yixian Yang

No matter where we are, we can post our feelings and ideas on Tumblr. Writing is a process to record what you are thinking and what your life looks like at any moment. We always have some great ideas suddenly pop up in our minds, so we need a convenient place to store what we are experiencing, seeing, and hearing. With Tumblr we can quickly share not only words and pictures but also videos. It is easy to learn how to make posts about what you are thinking. By using blogs to share valuable details in our daily lives, we may have more motivation to write down our thoughts without writer's block. Tumblr plays the role of an online diary, which is more convenient and easy for writing.

Before coming to the University of Alabama in Huntsville, we used Tumblr to share photos and fan pictures. Before taking English 101 with Studio, Tumblr was a place to share resources and personal feelings. It is not like blogs that require you to write long articles just like essays. Other blogs usually involve long articles about topics, but Tumblr is made for small posts, photos, and videos and for the sharing of ideas among followers.

We were surprised that we would be using Tumblr as a teaching approach in this course. In China we studied by ourselves, and few people would show their essays or work to others. Also, in our major courses and in courses like physics and chemistry, we can only do group work after class, so if you cannot meet after class, are shy, or don't know many classmates, it is hard to find peers to study with. Thus, it was all new to us to use Tumblr and peer review as a way to learn, and we felt curious about it.

In our studio class, when we posted on Tumblr we could take time writing down our thoughts and could share them without having to quickly speak in front of the class. It helped us practice our writing and our communication in English, and the time we spent online messaging peers helped make us more confident in talking with classmates from other classes. It was also a good place for brainstorming ideas for group projects. Tumblr made it easy to get more information through the Internet and brainstorm with our classmates by reblogging another's posts and adding our ideas to it.

We used Tumblr to write a few sentences or a paragraph centered on the topic the studio leader gave us. We could not take a long time to finish it because the assignment had a time limit. As a result we had to focus on writing only about the topic. We are used to taking a long time to write a lot of things; however, sometimes we go off topic. So we were a little unaccustomed to the timed assignments at the beginning. However, after several classes of it, we found that we could write faster and more tersely in a short time. Usually we would write a lot of foreshadowing or write something unrelated before we put forward what we thought. Aside from that, we did not know how to write our own feelings and ideas. Now our writing styles have changed, and we are able to state our thoughts straightforwardly and organize them in an appropriate sequence.

Publishing our ideas and thoughts on Tumblr helped us understand writing topics and assignments. When we first wrote about our rhetorical analysis essay, we could not figure out how to identify logos, ethos, and pathos, the three different ways of persuading. Our posts helped us, and they also helped our teacher to assess and judge whether we could distinguish the three. Sometimes in class, even if you don't understand, you will nod and plan on learning it later, but these activities let us practice and made sure we understood before moving on. Our teacher used Tumblr to give us a specific introduction to the material and some examples. We posted text, photo, or video examples of the three appeals and identified them in the comments when we reblogged others' posts. We also used Tumblr to express our understanding of these three appeals.

The most impressive part of the class for us was the peer review, because we had never done anything like that before taking this course. We could read our classmates' works and comment on them. We learned how to review other people's essays and take into account both their thoughts and our own. For example, once in a peer review about literacy narrative essays, a student wrote about how certain articles helped with her writing. It was a good idea, but she wrote only one and a half pages, so we suggested that she should write more details about what she experienced. We wrote about video games that helped us learn to read and speak English. She recommended that we should focus more on English games and how they affected our writing but that we should cut down some parts on the influences of other languages.

It was good advice that we might not have gotten in person, but because we were sharing ideas informally on Tumblr, everyone was more willing to give better advice.

If we write essays and only submit them to a teacher, we can receive only one set of comments. On Tumblr, however, we received different evaluations and even generated whole discussions. It helped us open our minds and learn from others in the class. Each person has his or her own writing style, and it is interesting and meaningful to know and recognize classmates' writing forms and styles. Then we can give better feedback the next time and point out to them the things they repeatedly do in their writing, like using the passive voice or the wrong tense.

Outside class work, by using Tumblr we made a lot of friends who have the same hobby we have. For instance, we are interested in watching *Gossip Girl*, so we focused on some blogs designed for the main actors and actresses in this TV series. Friends who are interested in Queen S and Queen B (two characters in *Gossip Girl*) can post from different parts of the world. We shared classic lines, enjoyed the fashion shown in the series, and added comments on one another's pictures and posts.

By using Tumblr to share thoughts online and by using group peer review, we learned how to communicate and work in groups with classmates from different backgrounds. Tumblr offered us a place to share our thoughts with classmates and listen to others' ideas. Our experience in this course influences us in other classes and in life. We can talk more bravely and directly with classmates and tutors. We also used to talk with our foreign friends only about daily life topics. Now more academic discussions are generated among us. We dare to put forward our thoughts in our major courses and set up study groups after class with our classmates because we are now more used to communicating with peers in English.

FAN ACTIVITIES IN ONLINE UNIVERSITY EDUCATION

Mattias Aronsson, Anneli Fjordevik, and Hiroko Inose

The fact that there are alternative ways of learning today and that the learning is "moving away" from the traditional classroom (Säljö, Lundgren, and Liberg 2014, 699) is presenting educational institutions with new prerequisites and challenges but also new possibilities. Learning today is "less and less a repetition of what is already known; it is more and more the production of something new, interesting, and relevant" (493). In this chapter we discuss possible ways of adapting fan activities on the Internet to academic-level online education. The study focuses on two types of fan activities: fan fiction and scanlation. The first is a form of creative writing based on existing works of art (e.g., novels, films, or other types of narratives), and the latter involves scanning and translating raw Japanese-style manga into other languages. In both cases, the works of the fans (in most cases amateurs, although they can be professionals as well) are uploaded onto the Internet for consumption by other fans, who can involve themselves in their creations by providing comments and feedback.

Since we teach Web-based courses only, we meet our students only in online synchronic seminars, not in person; thus the Web-based interaction is very central. This is also the case with fan communities. Our hypothesis is that connecting fan culture activities with the Web-based teaching of foreign languages may be a way to develop and improve the formal academic learning environment.[1]

The educational benefits of fan activities are mentioned by various authors. In *Convergence Culture*, Jenkins (2006a, 177) brings out "the informal pedagogy that emerged within the *Harry Potter* fan community," where both adults and children are involved and teach each other. Gee and Hayes (2011, 69) have come up with the concept of "passionate affinity-based learning" for the learning that "occurs when people organize themselves in the real world and/or via the Internet (or a virtual world) to learn something connected to a shared endeavor, interest, or passion." Olin-Scheller and Wikström (2010) have studied young people's writing in fan communities; however, they focus on teaching before university, until about eighteen or nineteen years of age, and their main objective is to inspire schoolteachers rather than university teachers.

FAN FICTION PROJECT DESIGN

The students of German and French literature are doing their first semester at the university level; however, before entering college, they have already studied the language in question at the secondary school level for at least a couple of years. This means that they can communicate quite well orally and that they are able to read and write in the foreign language (though not always with correct spelling or verb conjugation). Students in the course on modern German literature read nine books in German, whereas the students of French literature read six literary works in that language over the course of the semester. All books are discussed in small groups during online synchronic seminars (by means of the Adobe connect system used at Dalarna University).

The students receive questions to prepare before each seminar. The fan fiction exercise was conducted in the following way: Before the end of the academic course, the students were given an introductory class on the topic of fan fiction. They were then asked to choose one of the literary works studied during the semester and write a short story based on the chosen work. The text was to be written in the target language. Each student uploaded his or her text to the online learning platform (Fronter) and then received feedback from other members of the group. Finally, the students were asked to evaluate the exercise, individually and anonymously, by answering three questions in writing. They then put their answers in a forum on the platform. The questions in the evaluation focused on topics such as whether they enjoyed the activity, what they thought they learned from it, and what the peer feedback meant to them.

RESULTS

The semester in which we carried out our project (autumn 2014), there were fewer students than usual in the German literature course. Nine texts were uploaded on the learning platform Fronter. Most of the students (eight) chose to write about a short story: *Sonja* by Judith Hermann, *Die Tochter* or *Der Milchmann* by Peter Bichsel, or *Der Lehrer* or *Das Fenster-Theater* by Ilse Aichmann. Birgit Vanderbeke's novel *Das Muschelessen* was chosen by one student.

Four texts continued the original story, including two sequels to *Sonja*. In this original story, an anonymous narrator is torn between two women, the well-behaved Verena and the mysterious Sonja, and at the end of the story he decides to marry Verena. In one student text he misses his own wedding because he is looking for Sonja everywhere, and in another one he married Verena but has divorced her and is more alone than ever. Four other texts were told from another point of view. The narrator in *Das Muschelessen* is a seventeen-year-old girl. This turned into the point of view of her violent father, who is telling the story about his relationship with his mother. In a student text based on *Die Tochter*, a new person—a friend and colleague of the narrator—has been invented and is telling the story from her point of view, so the readers get to know things they previously did not know. One text on *Der Lehrer* added information about one of the protagonists, who acted strange in the original story. In the fan fiction text, we learn that he has an illness and as a result is very ashamed.

As stated earlier, the students of French literature had previously studied six literary works during the semester, and each text was chosen by at least one participant as a basis for the fan fiction activity. Thirty-two students uploaded a text on the online platform. *Le petit prince* (by Antoine de Saint-Exupéry) was the source of eleven fan fiction stories; *L'Amant* (by Marguerite Duras) was chosen by six students, and *Le Ventre de l'Atlantique* (by Fatou Diome) was chosen by another six. *Je voudrais que quelqu'un m'attende quelque part* (by Anna Gavalda) was preferred by five students, *Kiffe kiffe demain* (by Faïza Guène) by three, and *Huis clos* (by Jean-Paul Sartre) by one.

Popular variants on the fan fiction activity included the invention of a new ending to the original story (e.g., permitting the little prince and the aviator in *Le petit prince* to meet again, after the heartbreaking good-bye at the end of the original story), the filling of a gap in the original literary plot (e.g., introducing a new adventure for a character featured in *Kiffe kiffe demain*), and the presentation of the story from a different perspective (e.g., letting the Chinese man in *L'Amant* become the narrator so that the story can be told from his point of view). The students generally did very well with the creative aspect of the activity, and it was obvious that many participants, though not all (see the next section), enjoyed the free and creative type of writing that this exercise demanded. The quality of the formal aspects (e.g., spelling, verb conjugation) of the texts produced ranged from not completely satisfactory to very good. In most cases the quality was at least adequate, but eight students were asked to correct their texts' formal aspects and hand in a revised version.[2]

EVALUATION FEEDBACK

The students were asked to evaluate the fan fiction assignment by answering three questions: whether they enjoyed the assignment, whether they thought they had learned something from it, and how they felt about the feedback from other students. Most of the students of German literature who uploaded texts also responded to the evaluation. In general they were positive about this assignment. They enjoyed the creative element and the fact that it represented something new in the course, as we can see from comments like "it was a truly inspiring and creative task where the content is in the foreground and the language itself becomes secondary" and "I thought it was fun to write creatively and think of the stories in a new way."[3]

As for what the students learned, they mentioned language-related matters, such as new words and expressions. In this way the exercise was very instructive, according to the students, since they had to work with a dictionary at hand. Some of them also wrote about the creativity—that they learned (or rather, realized) that imagination can be practiced and improved by the use of creative tasks like these. One student reflected on the intertextuality of literature: "I have learned that literature can always continue and will do so. It is up to the readers to make something out of it, to be inspired."

Only a few students commented on the peer feedback. Both positive and negative reactions were found. One student wrote that "it is often feedback which makes the creation meaningful." Another student thought it was difficult to comment on another text ("What am I supposed to comment on? Language?").

In the French part of the survey, we received twenty-four answers to the question on whether they had enjoyed the fan fiction activity.[4] Thirteen students expressed only positive opinions, and eleven students highlighted both positive and negative aspects of the exercise. No one had a completely negative judgement. The positive opinions included formulations such as "it is nice to be given the opportunity to do something really creative," "the result makes you proud," and "I like to write but never find the time to do it, so I very much appreciate that it was a compulsory part of this course." The students who also mentioned negative aspects said, for instance, "I don't consider myself creative, and I lack practice when it comes to writing," "I feel I have no imagination and I am not very fond of writing fiction."

The question about the perceived learning outcomes of the activity generated some interesting comments. The students found that they learned new words and expressions in the target language, that they learned how to use dictionaries and conjugate verbs in different tenses, and that they realized they had to get a deeper understanding of the chosen work in order to write a text based on it. Some people appreciated the aspect of mimicry that was inherent in the activity; it was a nice experience, they said, to try to imitate the style of such distinguished authors as Duras or Saint-Exupéry.

When we asked for the students' opinions on the peer feedback they gave and received, we collected twenty-three answers. Eleven students conveyed only positive reactions, five expressed both positive and negative views, and seven had an overall negative opinion on this particular part of the activity. Those who appreciated the peer feedback said that it "was really nice to read the other students' texts," that "it was interesting to see how different the texts were, even when they dealt with the same subject matter," and that "I received useful comments, both on the content and on the formal aspects of the text." The negative reactions can be put into three categories: (1) some students found it difficult to comment on a text written in the target language and to give constructive feedback because they thought they lacked the necessary linguistic competence themselves, (2) some expressed reluctance to upload the text on the platform forum (open to all students in the course) and to give and receive feedback in this open venue, preferring to do this in smaller groups, and (3) a couple of students reacted to the fact that some participants received a lot of comments on their texts whereas others did not; this was not fair, they argued, to the participants whose contributions were more or less ignored.

SCANLATION PROJECT DESIGN

The fourteen students in the course Introduction to Translation (Japanese and English) were given the scanlation assignment as part of their course work. The level of Japanese language varied among the students, from intermediate to advanced. In order that the difficulty level of the text would be standardized, the teacher chose the manga text for translation: the first part of *Shissou Nikki* or *The Diary of a Disappeared* by Hideo Azuma). *Shissou Nikki*

(2005) is a nonfiction manga about an alcoholic manga artist who is himself the author. The popular manga artist Azuma one day disappears, escaping all his work commitments, and lives as a homeless man for several months until he is found and brought back home. The manga tells us how he lived his days as a homeless person.

Scanlators often work in groups, so the students were asked to form four groups (with a maximum of four members in each). The original material was then scanned and uploaded on the learning platform Fronter. Because the first part of *Shissou Nikki* contains an introduction and eight chapters (eight pages per chapter) that are serial but can be read independently, each group was assigned the translation of two chapters. The introduction was translated by the teacher and uploaded as an example.

Normally in scanlation, the original Japanese texts are eliminated in the speech bubbles so that the translated text can be put there. However, in this exercise, the students were recommended to use the sticky note function in Adobe Acrobat so that readers could read both the original and the translated texts at the same time. This allows students to check, analyze, and learn from the translation done by others rather than by reading only the finished translation. Groups were encouraged to discuss and decide on the best way to translate the original text and some translation problems specific to manga, such as onomatopoeic and mimetic words, as well as extra dialogues written directly in the panels or Japanese letters used in images (such as shop names, film posters, or station names).

The students were given three weeks to complete their scanlation and upload the chapters on Fronter for others to read and comment on. Each student was asked to read and comment on at least two chapters other than the chapters assigned to his or her group. In the class held after the exercise, each group was asked to have a short discussion about what its members thought about the exercise and what they had learned from it.

RESULTS

After the three weeks, eight chapters were uploaded to Fronter. Most of the groups used the sticky note function as recommended, except for one group, which chose to place its translated text in the bubbles as is done in the real scanlation situation.

The teacher did not correct any translations, and there were various minor mistranslations in all chapters, but no serious errors that might have changed the flow of the story. Considering the fact that the texts in manga are mostly dialogues written in spoken language with a great deal of grammatical and phonetic irregularities, as well as colloquial terms, the level of the translation achieved was quite satisfactory. The main causes of mistranslation were misinterpretation of subtle nuances (e.g., "*Mou koredake shika nai* [I have only very little left]" as "I have none") and cultural terms (e.g., *karakuchi* [not sweet] as "spicy"). Mistranslation could also happen when a narrative sentence was written over two consecutive panels but the students did not grasp this and translated them as two separate sentences. These types of misinterpretation and mistranslation can often be found in the works of real scanlation as well (Inose 2012, 80).

Furthermore, most of these errors were pointed out by students themselves when they commented on the chapters translated by other groups. In the real scanlation situation, the readers sometimes do leave comments for the scanlators, but they most often tend to thank them for their work and encourage them to make further scanlations. This could be partly because the readers normally see only the translated text in the scanlated versions, and even if it was possible to see both the original and the translation, most of the readers would not know Japanese, which is why they read a scanlated version in the first place. Discussions are held on forums for scanlators about possible interpretations and ways to translate subtle nuances or confusing terms, role languages (the use of language that shows one's gender, age, social class, and so on), and cultural terms in the original Japanese texts.

In the current assignment, those who commented were translators of other chapters, and since it was possible to see both the original and the translated texts and compare them, the comments were readers' reactions and also translators' discussions. In addition, the situation was not anonymous, as it would be in a real scanlation situation. The students had one week to submit their comments.

Most students congratulated the other groups on the naturalness of their translated texts, as well as on their use of various translation techniques learned in the course (such as the use of translator's notes or the way they dealt with cultural terms), but they also pointed out minor mistranslations and possible improvements for translated texts. From the teacher's point of view, the comments were very constructive indeed. The following are some examples of suggested points for improvement:

1. To translate, rather than to describe, all the onomatopoeic and mimetic words written within the panels. The comments suggested the possible translation of onomatopoeia and mimetic words that

appeared in the chapters, as well as the creation of neologisms when the equivalent terms did not exist in English.
2. To shorten the translated texts and translator's notes, since they would not fit within the bubble (in the case of dialogue) or the margin outside the panel (in the case of the translator's notes), and to suggest shorter versions of the texts.
3. To use cultural equivalence (e.g., "cooking oil" for *tempura oil*) rather than transference (i.e., to transcribe the foreign term) or to add a translator's note for certain cultural terms.
4. To use more natural spoken English, including some swear words, in order to reproduce the tone of the original texts. Here the comments normally suggested alternative translations.

These points reflect what the students had learned previously in the course, such as the appropriate use of various translation techniques.

Naturally, some of the mistranslations went unnoticed, and not all the changes suggested in the comments were necessary. However, the level of discussion (as well as translation) the students could achieve without the teachers' intervention was quite impressive in relation to the level of the course, which suggests a high level of engagement by students. This point will be discussed further in the next section.

EVALUATION FEEDBACK

In the class after the students had made all the required comments, the four groups had a short session (about fifteen minutes) to discuss three questions about the assignment. The questions were the same as for the fan fiction part of the project: did they enjoy the assignment, what did they learn, and how did they regard the importance of the peer review and comments.

The students were generally very positive about the assignment, and some students preferred it to all the other assignments in the course. Their enjoyment of the assignment was influenced by whether they liked the manga that they were to translate: this was clear from their comments. In the real scanlation situation, scanlators themselves choose which manga to translate. This is one of the limitations of the formal course assignment, in which the level of difficulty of the text has to be controlled by the teacher. However, the students considered the assignment to be a good opportunity for them to practice what they had learned in class, as well as to share knowledge, exchange ideas, and receive help within the group. It was the only group assignment in the course (the rest of the assignments were individual), and it was suggested that the course should have more such group assignments instead of individual assignments.

In terms of what they learned from the assignment, most of the groups mentioned ways to solve very concrete translation problems, such as the treatment of onomatopoeic and mimetic words or cultural terms. For this particular type of text (i.e., manga), the students understood that it is often preferable to translate these by using cultural equivalent terms, for example, than by explaining them with translator's notes, so that the flow of reading is not disturbed. Also, some groups pointed out that they learned to consider more than one perspective while working on the target text—that through collaboration, it was easier to see if an original text has been misinterpreted and to recognize that there was not just one correct version of the translation; rather, there could be many. Students also commented that through the compilation of various translated parts into one text, the input from all group members was made consistent, which made the students consider and discuss the best way to work with certain translation problems.

As for the importance of the comments, most groups pointed out the usefulness of recognizing their own mistranslations, missing parts, and possible improvements. Quite naturally, most groups focused on the function of comments as translators' discussions rather than readers' reactions and on the way they could be useful in the improvement of their own translation. However, one group also mentioned the importance of comments as readers' responses, pointing out that the activity of translation per se is carried out for the readers and not for the translators themselves, so it is extremely important that the translator receives the readers' responses.

DISCUSSION

Connecting fan culture activities to academic teaching is in line with some central thoughts of what learning is all about today (more genuine production and less repetition of what is already known). This seems to be a good way to develop and improve the formal academic learning environment in foreign languages, even though there is a fundamental difference between the re-creation of fan activities in the classroom and actual fan activities on the Internet: the word *fan* should here be used with some care, since most students are not de facto dedicated fans of the literature or manga they have to read or translate in a university course. They could, nevertheless, choose which book to use as a basis for the fan fiction assignment, and the element of creative writing made it stand out against most tasks that they are asked to do at the university.

Beside this difference, the necessity to control the activities to a certain extent (e.g., standardize the difficulty of the text to translate or choose what books to use as a basis for the fan fiction text) inevitably limits the extent to which we can repeat fan activities as classroom assignments. The anonymity is very central in both the creation and the commentary in fan communities. Since the teachers have to use grades in academia, they are not able to give the students anonymous assignments, and this fact, of course, influences what students write and how they comment. Some students of French literature (approximately one-third of those who completed the evaluation) were obviously uncomfortable with the peer feedback being received and given in such an open venue as the platform forum.[5]

One can, of course, wonder why there were so many participants who expressed negative opinions about this particular part of the assignment. Perhaps these individuals, quite simply, were not used to the participatory culture of the fan environment; perhaps it was a completely new experience for them to present their own material and comment on others' work in a Web-based community. These students may have felt unsure about how to deal with "netiquette"—the unwritten rules regulating interactions in a Web-based environment—or perhaps it was the lack of anonymity that spurred the negative reactions, in this case.

In fan communities, we also often find the function of a beta reader: a person who reads and comments on the text or checks the quality of the translation before the publication. We did not offer this function in our assignments this semester, but the teacher could very well choose to do so—for instance, by pairing students and letting them give feedback on each other's work, before the texts are uploaded on the platform. Another fact that may have influenced the students' writing in the fan fiction assignment is the language issue. They were supposed to write in German or French, a language that is their second or even third foreign language. People writing fan fiction normally write either in their mother tongue or in English.

These points can be seen as limitations, since we cannot completely imitate a real fan situation. The presence of the "passionate affinity-based learning" (Gee and Hayes 2011, 71–72) that was mentioned at the beginning of the chapter can therefore be discussed, but the students can still benefit from such aspects as interaction, collaboration, and creative writing, since these important features are, in fact, closely tied to the fan-based activities described here. As Jenkins (2006b, 19) put it, the "new literacies almost all involve social skills developed through collaboration and networking." If old forms of expertise are rather isolated disciplines, the term *collective intelligence*, which was introduced by Pierre Lévy (1997) can be seen as a "patchwork woven together from many sources as members pool what they know, creating something much more powerful than the sum of its parts" (Jenkins 2006b, 140).

As noted, the attempt to repeat the fan activities within a formal learning environment can have its limitations. However, it is also true that these assignments were received positively by most of the students. From their feedback, we can see that the students believed that they had practiced various skills, some directly related to the course contents, others more general. For example, in the fan fiction assignments, students felt they needed to have a deeper understanding of the original texts in order to create different but convincing endings. It was also necessary for them to analyze the original styles in order to imitate them. Sometimes the need to "continue" or to "see the different side" of the story made them think about literary concepts, such as narratology and intertextuality. In the case of the scanlation assignment, working in groups and knowing that their translation was going to be read by the rest of the class (or that it would have "readers") seemed to enable them to interpret the original text more accurately and to consider various possible techniques for solving the identified translation problems. Later, in their comments on others' translations, their skills in the area of translation criticism were used fully – not only to point out the mistranslations but also to make suggestions on how to improve the translation. These concrete skills were practiced because they were all necessary. One thing we may notice is the wide range of skills that are required for students to complete this type of "less controlled" assignment.

Compared with those assignments we usually use in our courses, fan activity assignments require a greater deal of creativity, as well as collaboration and knowledge sharing (both when working in groups and when commenting on others' work). The collective intelligence and social skills, which might be regarded as more general skills that can be acquired by participating in the fan activities, seem to be present in those copied environments as well.

As it turned out, the fan fiction assignment proved to be a useful tool for the teachers inasmuch as it helped them decide whether the students had reached the goals of the course. Goals such as "after the course, the student should be able to read and interpret a selection of literary texts," "the student should be able to use a relevant vocabulary in writing," and "the student should be able to reflect on his or her own learning process" can, in fact, be achieved by the means of such an assignment as the fan fiction exercise in this project.[6] The students can attain the first two goals by successfully accomplishing the fan fiction exercise itself, and the third goal is closely linked to the subsequent online seminar, during which the exercise is evaluated and students are asked to reflect on their own learning process. In one way, therefore, what students can achieve in fan activity–based assignments can fit very well within the formal learning environment.

One challenge for the teacher with the scanlation exercise is the fact that the students work in small groups with the assignment, yet they are also supposed to be marked individually. This is, of course, a difficulty inherent in all kinds of group-oriented work, which might indicate the limitation of the current course designs within a formal learning environment, which makes it very difficult to evaluate the use of collective intelligence, for example. The teacher in this project chose not to grade the students individually on this particular assignment. However, since such a grading *must* be done on the course as a whole (according to university regulations), the teacher has to give complementary assignments in which the students' individual achievements can be identified.

CONCLUSION

Our attempt to apply fan culture activities on the Web-based teaching of foreign languages has proven that the students could very well fulfill the goals of the courses (as they are expressed in the syllabus). Although arranging the systems of spontaneous learning to fit into a more formal learning environment has its obvious difficulties, these activities are definitely pertinent to the process of learning defined as "the production of something new, interesting and relevant" (Säljö 2004, 493).

The collaborative element—most visible in the scanlation assignment but also present in the fan fiction exercise—is an important prerequisite of learning, according to the advocates of the sociocultural perspective on learning (e.g., Säljö 2000; 2015, 89–107). When the students work together and help each other with the assignment, they are able to share knowledge and learn from one another. Therefore, the most important learning outcome of the exercises described in this project may very well be that the students *learn how to learn* in an effective way.

NOTES FOR CHAPTER 6

1. At Dalarna University (Sweden), which specializes in online education, a three-year project called Informal Learning Environment explored the educational aspects of fan activities and the possible ways to apply them in foreign-language (French, German, Japanese, and Portuguese) and literature courses.

2. In this case, *adequate* refers to a piece of work in which the quality of the formal aspects is at least acceptable. This does not mean that the text must be flawless—after all, it is written in a foreign language by a student doing his or her first year at the university. However, the text cannot contain too many formal errors if it is to be accepted by the teacher.

3. All quotations from the evaluation of the fan fiction exercise have been translated by the authors. The students wrote their assessment in the target language or in Swedish.

4. The evaluation was done during the online synchronic seminar that followed the fan fiction exercise. Twenty-seven students attended this seminar, which means that three participants chose not to take part in the evaluation. The response rate was therefore rather high, 89 percent.

5. In the evaluation, they wrote, for instance, "I didn't feel competent enough to comment on other persons' language" and "It is hard to know if a person appreciates critical feedback or not—I would have preferred to give my comments more privately" (our translation, from the target language or Swedish).

6. The goals are quoted from the syllabus at Dalarna University (our translation).

TEACHING DECONSTRUCTION USING FAN VIDS

Shannon K. Farley

As a fan scholar who is writing her dissertation on the history of rewriting, I have been building an argument for some time for the power of fan work as textual criticism. I've been watching vids and following vidders for even longer. Fans of vids have long recognized that some videos succeed in showing their audiences a side of the source text that they had never seen before. Barry (2002), whose text I used with my junior year writing class for comparative literature majors, states that a deconstructive reading aims to produce disunity—to show that what had appeared to be a coherent text is in fact unstable and contradictory. This is the major characteristic of a deconstructive reading. Vids often enact these very kinds of deconstructive readings.

For undergraduate literature majors, the theory of deconstruction is often quite challenging even as other styles of literary criticism come easily. For this reason, I felt the need to develop a lesson that made the abstract nature of deconstruction as concrete as possible. The visual quality of deconstructive videos made the act of deconstructive reading as concrete as I could make it in the classroom.

Vidding as an aspect of fan culture dates back to 1975, when college student and *Star Trek* club member Kandy Fong first set a slideshow of static images from *Star Trek* to music during a fan convention. Since that time, both the technology used to make vids and the messages vidders wish to send with their work have evolved. Some vids celebrate certain characters or story lines, some serve as recruitment tools to convince other fans to join a fandom, and some take a more critical stance in relation to their source texts. Coppa (2008, 1) notes that "fannish vidders use music in order to comment on or analyze a set of preexisting visuals. . . . In vidding, the fans are fans of the visual source, and music is used as an interpretive lens to help the viewer to see the source text differently. A vid is a visual essay that stages an argument, and thus it is more akin to arts criticism than to traditional music video." That urge to critique, the visual nature of fan vids, and the pop culture source texts make fan vids excellent examples of textual criticism in an undergraduate classroom.

As part of a university-wide writing program, junior year writing exists to build on a basic undergraduate writing class and instruct upperclass students on writing in their chosen fields of study. When I teach junior year writing for the comparative literature majors at the University of Massachusetts at Amherst, I begin with six weeks of instruction and practice in the schools of literary criticism. Utilizing the tools of literary criticism is the main mode of writing in comparative literature, but many of my students are still unfamiliar with them by the time they reach their junior year. Thus I need to approach them in an introductory fashion. To do so, I combine traditional readings about the schools of literary criticism in Peter Barry's *Beginning Theory* with concrete examples in media other than the traditional literature with which comparative literature majors are already familiar. This combination has proven successful in engaging the students in some unfamiliar theoretical activity.

After a week of introducing the class and theory in general, and then a week on structuralism, we arrive at deconstruction and poststructuralism. Deconstruction is generally held to be one of the more difficult schools of literary criticism to teach. I frequently recall with discomfort my own attempts to understand Jacques Derrida's writing as a sophomore philosophy student. Peter Barry uses Dylan Thomas's poem "A Refusal to Mourn the Death, by Fire, of a Child in London" as his case study in deconstruction, and although he does an adequate job, my students generally don't find it as engaging as deconstructive analysis has the potential to be.

The word *deconstruct* has become popular, especially within the industries of food and fashion—and in that context has basically come to simply mean "to take apart." Dresses and dishes are deconstructed and presented as simply a pile of parts. This is not what Derrida meant to do when he called for a kind of reading that critiques itself. To truly be deconstructive a critique must read, in Eagleton's (1986) words, "against the grain" of the source. It should argue against not only the source's own sense of itself but also the structures and authorities on which it bases its assumptions. The level at which I am teaching deconstructive critique is rather introductory, so we do not make strong distinctions among deconstruction, poststructuralism, and postmodernism. At this very basic level, however, it is clear to my students that what we are after is a kind of self-aware structuralism, a recognition that both narrative and meaning are artificially constructed. Derrida himself refused to define *deconstruction*, and he repeatedly said that to attempt to do so was to miss the point.

However, at this time in the history of literary criticism, we can identify a starting point, at the very least, for doing deconstructive critique. As Barry (2002, 72) defines it, deconstructive critique "aims to show that the text is at war with itself.... The deconstructionist looks for evidence of gaps, breaks, fissures and discontinuities of all kinds." This also means that a deconstructive critique often uncovers an unconscious dimension of the text, destabilizing it by questioning the normative assumptions that serve as its central structure. For our purposes, this means that deconstruction can often intersect with feminist, queer, Marxist, or postcolonial critique.

Within this six-week unit we spend one or two class days on each school of literary criticism. After each school is introduced, the students practice using the tools of critique—sometimes on a text of their choice and other times on an assigned text. During the week that we discuss feminist criticism and psychoanalytic criticism, for example, I screen an episode from the third season of *Mad Men*, and the students are free to choose one or both of those schools as the perspective from which they analyze the episode. When we get to deconstruction, I spend an entire class period screening a curated vid show. I begin by acknowledging that, at first glance, all fan vids—or any remix do-it-yourself videos, for that matter—may appear to be deconstructive, since they take apart footage from their source texts and reconstruct it to create something new. However, in order to get at the distinction between structuralism and deconstruction, I need to be able to show them that a truly deconstructive vid creates a new narrative that argues something that the source text either never intended or never consciously acknowledged.

My vid show begins with *Handlebars* by Seah and Margie, two fans who vid together under the name flummery. *Handlebars* is a Doctor Who vid set to the song of the same name by Flobots. I use it precisely not because it is a deconstructive vid but because it is making a very structuralist argument. The topic of the vid is the development of the Tenth Doctor's personality over the course of the second, third, and fourth seasons of the show. The song sets up a progression that begins with innocence and eventually and inevitably leads to death and destruction. The protagonist in the narrative of the song tells a story of increasing power corresponding with increasing violence. "I can ride a bike with no handlebars," he proudly begins, as the vid shows us the Doctor playfully catching his sonic screwdriver while hanging off the Empire State Building. Eventually the song's protagonist's power becomes greater and greater. The vid shows us the Doctor with his typically good intentions and superior experience becoming a person who, as the lyrics to the song suggest, can imprison those he dislikes, and there are corresponding images of Harriet Jones, the prime minister, in the moment that the Doctor decides he is going to destroy her career. The climax of the vid comes as Flobots sing about having the ability to destroy the world while images are displayed of the violence that always seems to follow the Doctor, even as he fights against it.

I call this vid structuralist because the argument it is making is textual. The show *Doctor Who* makes the same argument as the vid, on some level. Various characters quite frequently challenge the Doctor's assumption that his "power is pure"—including Harriet Jones, who is punished specifically for acting to protect the planet without the doctor's approval. It is a very well-organized, powerful vid, but it is not arguing against the grain of the source text; it is making a particularly well-focused argument about what the show itself is saying. Once my students understand this, it becomes easier for them to recognize in other vids an argument that demonstrates a disunity within the source text.

The first vid that I usually show them in my progression of deconstructive vids is mresundance's *Whole New Way*. Stein and Busse (2012, 9) suggest that this vid "proposes that the recent incarnations of Sherlock offer avenues of fan devotion and investment that may seem new because of their location within digital culture, but in fact have long histories in Sherlock Holmes fandom and in the original Arthur Conan Doyle narratives." The vid absolutely does this, and it does so through a kind of postmodern self-awareness that deconstructs the processes of fandom as much as or more than it deconstructs the source text itself. It also "queers" the texts—not only the BBC's *Sherlock*, Guy Ritchie's *Sherlock Holmes* film, and Arthur Conan Doyle's Sherlock Holmes stories, but also the fandom itself. In contrast to *Handlebars*, *Whole New Way* is almost entirely subtextual, and on many different levels.

The song to which *Whole New Way* is set is the Scissor Sisters track of the same name. This song choice is packed with significance. The Scissor Sisters are well known as a band that emerged from the gay club scene, and the song is overtly sexual. The vid combines suggestive lyrics with suggestive cuts from the various sources. Thus on one level *Whole New Way* is a classic slash vid, arguing for a queer relationship between Sherlock Holmes and John Watson in all their incarnations. At the same time, however, the vid intercuts the subtextual suggestions with images of fandom activity. There are screencaps of the Sherlock BBC LiveJournal community discussion of "Holmes/Watson in Bed," for example, paired with an illustration from the Arthur Conan Doyle text that depicts just that and intercut with Robert Downey Jr. resting his head on Jude Law's shoulder and Benedict Cumberbatch winking at Martin Freeman. The point of view of the protagonist in the narrative of the song, therefore, becomes an unstable perspective switching back and forth from Holmes and Watson to fandom itself. As the vid progresses, the lyric "we can talk about relationships, but there's better things to fill your head with" pairs with looks between the respective Holmeses and Watsons, moves to a naked and tied-up Robert Downey Jr., Benedict Cumberbatch using a whip on a corpse, and a screenshot of the header for the LiveJournal community sherlockbbc_fic, which at the time called itself "Sherlock Kink." In this series of images, it is almost impossible to tell who the *we* is and who the *you* is, but that is precisely the point.

The effect of this vid on my students is always incredibly interesting. They pick up on the queer subtext first, almost unanimously. The next layer of the vid, in which the voice is not necessarily that of Holmes or Watson but of the fans who have found whole new ways to love the characters, takes more exploration for us to unearth. Once we do, the distinction between a structuralist vid like *Handlebars* and a postmodern one like *Whole New Way* becomes much more clear. It is precisely this self-aware quality that marks this vid as not only deconstructive but postmodern.

If any students come away from *Whole New Way* without a complete understanding of the queering power of slash vids, they have a much more thorough idea after the next vid in the show, talitha78's *Tonight I'm F—king You*. A vid of the TV series *White Collar* that focuses on the relationship of FBI agent Peter Burke and white-collar criminal–turned–FBI consultant Neal McCaffery, *Tonight I'm F—king You* can be characterized as a straight-up classic slash vid. According to Turk and Johnson (2012), there exists a classic fannish trope of two people—frequently two men—who "don't seem to get along but fall in love anyway" (4.7). Turk and Johnson are describing a different vid for their case study but within a larger discussion of the ecology of vidding: the system of production in which fans act "as readers, writers, vidders, vid watchers, posters, commenters, lurkers, essayists, artists, icon makers, recommenders, coders, compilers of images and links, users and maintainers of archives and other fannish infrastructures, and so on" (2012, 2.3). Because I cannot count on my students being previously familiar with fannish systems—indeed, even the students who identify as fans are often not familiar with the particular subsection of fandom that takes vidding as seriously as the fans I feature in this vid show—they miss many of the cues and tropes that another fan may see. It is for this reason that *Tonight I'm F—king You* is such a particularly good example of deconstructive queering. It is not subtle—neither in its choice of song nor in its choice of clips.

Enrique Iglesias sings the song from the point of view of a young man who is addressing the object of his desire. After one long breathy "you" begins the song, he croons that he knows that the person in question desires him as well. In the hands of talitha78, the narrative is one of consensual, mutual desire. Peter and Neal exchange multiple intimate looks, smiles, and suggestive gestures—including the fondling of a pen. The original song, however, gives the object of the protagonist's desire no voice and indeed no agency. "Excuse me, I don't mean to be rude, but tonight I'm f—king you," is the repeated chorus. On the face of it, this song is extremely problematic as one of a series of examples of pop songs in which a woman is reduced to a sexual object. In the official video of the radio version, "Tonight I'm Loving You," Iglesias broods over and has sex with a horde of women whom he appears to have picked up in clubs. In contrast, talitha78's vid makes an argument that a long-standing, intimate, playful relationship between two men is also sexual. The intimacy and the playfulness of the two leads of *White Collar* is textual. The sexual nature of that relationship is not. Additionally, this vid succeeds in deconstructing the song by destabilizing the voices of sexual subject and sexual object. Because both actors in the vid are male, it is difficult to argue definitively which one of their points of view is meant to be that of the singer at any given time. In this way, it subverts the text of the song as well as the structural sexism of pop songs in general.

From deconstructive queering, the class vid show proceeds to class structures. *Telephone*, a vid by fahrbot_drusilla, combines the points of view of the movie characters Batman (*Batman Begins*) and Rorschach (*Watchmen*), using the song of the same name by Lady Gaga and Beyoncé. *Telephone* functions as a comparative analysis of the characters of Batman and Rorschach, and I argue that it focuses specifically on their similarities while also highlighting their major difference: social class.

As the song begins, Lady Gaga sings to someone on the other end of her telephone that she cannot hear, and we see that both Bruce Wayne/Batman and Walter Kovacs/Rorschach are emotionally detached from people who care about them. "Sorry I cannot hear you, I'm kinda busy" repeats several times as the beat picks up, and Batman and Rorschach each go to work as his respective city's masked vigilante. As the lyric of the song repeats Lady

Gaga's desire to stop talking and start dancing, we are treated to scenes of Batman and Rorschach fighting that are so masterfully cut together that it becomes difficult to tell where one source's footage leaves off and the next one begins. The two men's childhoods are set in parallel, and we see the connections between past trauma and present violence for both of them. However, Rorschach's mother is a prostitute and his childhood is one of abject poverty, whereas Batman's parents are killed in the street by a mugger while dressed for the opera—marking them as wealthy.

At another point the vid pairs footage from both sources that take place inside a prison. Other differences can be seen here, for Rorschach is an inmate in these scenes whereas Batman is not. The narrative moves Batman out of the prison and into a tuxedo making a champagne toast as Bruce Wayne. Rorschach remains in the prison but ultimately breaks out with the help of Nite Owl and Silk Spectre. At the conclusion of the vid (as well as the films), Rorschach is dead and Batman is not. Nite Owl and Silk Spectre look mournfully at the Rorschach blot left on the snow while Bruce Wayne watches his childhood love, Rachel Dawes, walk away from him. Although both men have sacrificed relationships for their vigilantism, only Rorschach pays with his life.

The argument of *Watchmen* as a text—especially the original comic series by Alan Moore—is that of the problematic nature of superheroes, but the argument of this vid goes further by matching it with a particular incarnation of a particular superhero and deconstructing them both. For students familiar with *Batman Begins*, *Watchmen*, or both, this is a potent argument. For those who are not, this vid at least opens up the discussion of deconstructing texts in terms of class structure and gives us an opportunity to connect to forms of Marxist criticism. At the very least, I can see a spark of recognition in my students' eyes when I argue that Batman's superpower is money.

The next vid in this lecture is *Women's Work*, by sisabet and Luminosity, set to Hole's song "Violet." *Women's Work* has already been the subject of a fair amount of analysis, for it is one of the most powerful feminist vids to have emerged from fandom. Hill (2007, 2) interviewed Luminosity, who described the critical work she and sisabet were doing with *Women's Work*: "*Women's Work* is a critique of the eroticization of the violence done to women in all media, not just *Supernatural*. Women are sexually assaulted, murdered, and then laid out in artistic tableaux, chopped into pretty, bloody pieces. They usually further the plot, but they're hardly ever a part of the plot. We wanted to point out that in order for us to love a TV show—and we do—we have to set this horrible part of it aside."

As a deconstructive analysis, *Women's Work* is brilliant. Every image is of a female character from *Supernatural* in either the role of victim or the role of demon, and each one of them is eroticized. Paired with Hole's angry feminist lyrics, the effect is breathtaking. "They get what they want, and they never want it again" repeats, along with images of women with cut throats, with broken necks, and burning on the ceiling, pinned by supernatural forces.

As a pedagogical tool, *Women's Work* is almost unparalleled. The argument is highly structured. There are almost no instances of the main male characters in the vid. Instead, the misogyny that is always in the background in *Supernatural* is thrust to the foreground as each image of sexualized violence against women is set beside the last. In our discussion, we point out that this is not unlike building a critical argument with choice quotes from the source text. The strength of the argument of *Women's Work* is overwhelming because of the number and relevance of each of its "quotes." *Women's Work* is obviously arguing against the grain of *Supernatural*, pointing out that the cumulative effect of every instance of sexualized violence results in a text that is even more of a horror show than the text could ever intend. In its own context, *Women's Work* exploded the binaries within *Supernatural* fandom. Freund (2010) describes the effect of watching *Women's Work* as a *Supernatural* fan as follows:

> It so clearly deconstructs the representations of women throughout the source material and highlights the series' (mis)treatment of its female characters that suddenly I was watching *Supernatural* in a whole new light, and one that was not necessarily favorable. During season 3, in particular, I struggled with my newfound relationship with the source material after watching what has become the most controversial episode, 3.09 "Malleus Maleficarum." I sought out episode reviews on LiveJournal for the first time to see if other fans shared my reactions and discovered a maelstrom of negative commentary: not only were fans incensed with the series and its writers, but they were also arguing with each other. (1.5)

The structures of sexism and misogyny in the wider media culture and the disunity inherent in a majority-female fandom for a show that embraces (whether consciously or unconsciously) so much eroticized violence ultimately cannot hold up, especially against such a skilled deconstruction. The few times that I have had *Supernatural* fans in the class when I show this vid, they cannot help but acknowledge that the argument made by *Women's Work* is undoubtedly accurate. The discomfort that ensues when one is nonetheless a fan of such a problematic text can lead to a very fruitful discussion—both in fandom and in class.

Our final vid is another well-known deconstructive vid with an especially postcolonial perspective. *How Much Is That Geisha in the Window?* is a vid of the fan favorite *Firefly* television series set to an instrumental song from the soundtrack to the movie *Ravenous*. The vidder, Lierdumoa, summarizes it in the original post on her journal: "Fuck you Joss, you racist asshole—an ode to the invisible Asians of Firefly." Lierdumoa's vid remixes and recontextualizes the visuals of *Firefly*, bringing what is background into the foreground. She focuses on the Asian extras, the Chinese-influenced dress and rituals of the Companions (analogues of geishas in the series), and then ends the vid with the following text on the screen: "There is only one Asian actor with English dialogue in all of *Firefly*. She plays a whore." The vid then plays audio of much of the Chinese dialogue from the show, followed by a voice-over: "Fuck you Joss, you racist asshole." The Joss in question is Joss Whedon, the executive producer of *Firefly* and the creative force behind many other fan favorites, including *Buffy the Vampire Slayer* and *The Avengers*.

Firefly is most commonly described as a "space-western." It takes place five hundred years in the future, when the United States and China have formed an alliance and a "corporate supergovernment." Whedon (Huddleston 2002) explains the origin of the series as follows:

> I read *The Killer Angels*. The minutia of the Battle of Gettysburg and the lives of the people in it really made *Firefly* just pop out of my head. I want to get into people's lives this intimately. I want to do it in the future and show that the future is the past. So I built the structure of the world and the look of the show on the Reconstruction Era. . . . We based a lot of things on the Civil War and the 1880s stylistically. We mixed it up with a lot of different cultures. There are a lot of Chinese in their outfits and their culture and their language. Every working-class American-seeming person speaks Chinese as well, because these are the two big powers. The idea is [that] they are the Alliance—the powerful government that our hero fought against. They're not the bad guys. They're just representative of the big government who sometimes comes in and makes things better, and sometimes they come in and [mess] everything up. Just like real big governments do.

The series has an ensemble cast of nine main characters—a very large cast by television standards. Whedon addresses this directly in the interview by explaining how much "richer" the stories become when there are so many people in the show whom the audience cares about.

However, in a world that he creates as being heavily influenced by Chinese culture, not a single member of the large ensemble cast is Chinese, or even Asian. There are a great many Asian extras and much Asian "flavor" to the sets of the series, but the elements of the show that are Chinese are merely background details. Lierdumoa's vid highlights this fact, as well as the parallels between the Browncoat protagonists of *Firefly* and the Confederacy. Lierdumoa adds footage from *Gone with the Wind* to make this parallel even more obvious. The purely instrumental music is eerie—no unsurprise, since it comes from a film about cannibalism. One is left with an uneasy feeling as well as a more acute awareness of the ways in which *Firefly* is decorated with Asianness much more than it engages with it. Lierdumoa's structure, like sisabet and Luminosity's, is very focused. There is very little of the actual main cast in the vid. The transitions between the clips from *Firefly*, *Memoirs of a Geisha*, *3:10 to Yuma*, and *Gone with the Wind* are seamless. The fact that one cannot tell where one film's footage ends and the next begins supports Lierdumoa's argument about the message of all these texts.

Whether students are in agreement about the problematic nature of *Firefly*'s appropriation of Asian culture or *Supernatural*'s use of gendered violence, these vids are able to make a convincing argument in a short amount of time. Watching them in their variety through the course of one lecture period helps students sense the diversity of postmodern thought. As a pedagogical tool, nothing else can encapsulate the nature of deconstructive analysis with such power in such a short amount of time. This particular lesson has been highly successful in instructing undergraduate literature majors in both the theory and practice of deconstruction. For the three semesters that I have taught this class, the writing assignment has been a short response paper to either a specific vid or the practice of vidding in general. In these response papers, the students have engaged with the arguments made by particular vids, reflecting on the strength of the arguments. They have also marveled at the practice of vidding in general and discussed their personal growth in recognizing the legitimacy of this kind of analysis. Although I cannot ask them to execute their own vids in a writing class, in future classes I would like to ask that the students think on a particular deconstructive argument they'd like to make about a visual source text and explain how they might go about creating a vid to argue it. In this way, they will both practice deconstruction and think more deeply about the analytical skills that go into producing a well-constructed fan vid.

REACTING TO (RE)EDITS

A Student's Experience with Vids

John Sanders

My understanding of fan-made videos ("vids") before entering Shannon Farley's junior year writing class was at about the same level as my understanding of deconstruction, the concept the vids would be used to teach. I had heard of both, and I understood neither. To me, vids were celebrations of a particular piece of media. Selecting the right music to go along with a collection of clips or finding similar scenes in multiple media and splicing them together for comedic effect was about as critical as the process went. That was the impression I got from vidder bironic's *Starships*, which was basically a compilation of famous science-fiction starship crews dogfighting, hitting warp speed, and throwing themselves from side to side hilariously whenever the ship got hit, all set to a catchy Nikki Minaj song. When asked to define the argument behind such a work, the classroom of amateur literary theorists became silent as they flipped through their mental notes of Jacques Derrida and Roland Barthes. Only when a solitary voice ventured, "Spaceships are cool?" did the room relax and settle into the all-too-obvious truth. The collection of clips with music accompaniment was not exactly the pinnacle of critical discourse, at least not in this case. As we would see, however, the simplicity of the form conceals a huge amount of deconstructive potential.

One of the vids that stood out to me was the third vid we were shown: talitha78's *Tonight I'm F—king You*, a mash-up of the television series *White Collar* set to the racy Enrique Iglesias song of the same name. The vid attempts to intimate a sexual relationship between the two main characters through a rapid-fire montage of suggestive microinteractions from the show's early seasons. Even though I had never seen *White Collar*, I knew this to be an exaggerated and noncanonical claim in the context of the show's narrative, but the vid's portrayal destabilized my belief in that authority. When gathered together from their original contexts, all the "come-hither" looks, raised eyebrows, smiles, and even phallic imagery between the two well-dressed male leads make a good case for the existence of the relationship the song extolls. All the moments in the vid could be easily overlooked while watching the show, but the reproduction of them in the vid served a "zoom and enhance" function, making the viewer realize just how common these flirtations were and revealing the internal contradiction within the work, the "repressed unconscious within [its] language" (Barry 2002, 68).

This decentralization of meaning caused some discomfort among my peers and me, causing one student to protest, "But that's not in the show. It's not really what happened." That was never the point: the vidder's process of queering this text was not meant to speculate on what *could* happen canonically, but to produce a new meaning from the elements he or she saw. That was what resonated with me: vidding, like deconstruction, is a creative process, forming a new interpretation from an already-existing work. This new text is as intimately linked to the source text as a house is with the materials that were used to build it; if there was no evidence to support it, the argument would not stand.

The idea of deconstruction as a creative process was driven home by the last vid we watched in class: Lierdumoa's *How Much Is that Geisha in the Window?*, based on the space-western *Firefly*. Set to music that mixes disjointed pluckings on an Eastern chord progression with a wheezing accordion, the vid scrolls through multiple representations of the Asian characters in *Firefly*—all of which seem oversexualized, exotified, or just downright racist (e.g., a sign over a meat shop proclaiming "good dog" appears multiple times). This message is brought home as triumphant horns join the track just as the American cowboyesque characters ride in on horses, guns blazing. The commentary at the end of the vid decrying this racist and colonialist attitude is almost unnecessary: by condensing all the problematic parts of the entire series into a three-minute window, Lierdumoa successfully creates a strong postcolonial deconstruction of the source material in a way only a vid can. Because I am a fan of the show, my gut instinct was to explain away the problematic representations the vid made abundantly clear by somehow claiming that the strong characters and great dialogue outweighed the much less frequent failings, or even that the moments in the vid were invalid when taken out of context. Yet as a work of such destabilizing evidence, the vidder's interpretation could not be repressed. The disunity of the narrative—a futuristic society that is built on an uncritical acceptance of present-day racist stereotypes—pulled authority away from the show's director and toward the vidder, who dismantled reality with little more than some editing software and a song. This is the true power of deconstructive criticism, and I found it downright inspiring.

Since Shannon's class, I have carried this mindset into almost every aspect of my academic career. My current (and future) research lies in video games, a medium abundant with issues of representation in race, class, sex, gender, and many others. It should come as no surprise that the damsel is saved too often or that the majority of the enemies in your crosshairs have dark skin, but these details are commonly missed in the context of play. In fact, as scandals like Gamer Gate have recently revealed to the gaming world, these charges are often vehemently denied by those who do not understand the process of authority and meaning making in a poststructuralist context. By revealing the inherent instabilities in the games we play, we might reveal the tenuous nature of the authority that underlies these problematic representations in the same way vids do: through editing and context. The process has already begun, as vloggers (video bloggers) splice game footage and designers question the underlying mechanics of the form. To me, deconstruction is the main weapon in this new battlefield; it gives Derrida's notion of free play a new (literal) meaning. Perhaps as I pursue my studies, I will be able to design a deconstructive game of my own.

"YOU DO REALIZE *THE LION KING* IS SET IN AFRICA, RIGHT?"

Utilizing Fan Studies to Teach about Race and Racism in the University Classroom

Rukmini Pande

At the outset it will be useful to clarify the referents of the terms I use in this chapter. There are, of course, many kinds of fans and fan communities, but my focus is on what is broadly termed as media fandom—that is, communities of fans that interact with popular cultural texts in various ways to produce and consume transformative fanworks (Hills 2002; Jenkins 1992; Penley 1992). These fan works take multiple forms—fan art, fan vids, fan fiction, and so on—and are generally circulated today through Internet-enabled platforms and networks. Although these are transnational communities, and fanworks are produced in multiple languages as well, for the purposes of this chapter I focus on English-language fan communities that draw from popular cultural texts produced mainly in the United States and the United Kingdom. It should also be noted that media fandom has consistently been identified as a space with a high degree of participation by women, many of whom identify as queer in some way (Busse, Lothian, and Reid 2007; Centrumlumina 2013).

ACTIVE AUDIENCES: FANDOM IN THE CLASSROOM

At present, in line with the larger mainstreaming of fan cultures, these fan works are increasingly being integrated in tertiary pedagogical practices as educators work to engage students through their interest in widely recognizable popular cultural texts and tropes. Some teachers also hope to leverage the participatory nature and transformative potential of fan communities in order to encourage the critical faculties of students. Fan studies remains a remarkably interdisciplinary field, drawing from disciplines such as gender and queer studies, communication studies, and popular culture studies, as well as offering insights into diverse issues from copyright law to language learning to online privacy. It is therefore inevitable that the application of fan practices to classroom learning has been just as varied. Indeed, the wide scope of the chapters in this collection itself demonstrates the diverse approaches that may be taken toward accomplishing this task.

A quick survey of the field shows that so far, fan-based pedagogical strategies have focused largely on fan texts as exemplars of participatory and/or critical activity that may be studied at a distance from the communities that produce it (Black 2008a; Gutiérrez 2011; Stedman 2012). This is a result of multiple factors, perhaps the most crucial of which are concerns for fan privacy and the desire of educators (who are often fans themselves) to shield those communities from being "outed" to the mainstream. Indeed, in 2015 an undergraduate class on fan fiction at the University of California–Berkeley attracted widespread condemnation within English-language media fandom for failing to pay adequate attention to communitarian norms of communication by instructing students to critique fan fiction stories directly on the platforms where they were hosted. This caused a certain amount of distress to authors who were unused to getting feedback in such a format and tone on their work. Although the class in question turned out to be an informal one led by undergraduates (which explained the lack of institution of ethical safeguards), the case is emblematic of the friction sometimes caused by academic interactions with fandom communities, especially in dynamic environments like the classroom (Baker-Whitelaw 2015).

Although this incident may be taken as a warning sign for educators to further divorce their teaching practices from fandom communities, focusing even more on discrete texts rather than the environment in which they are produced, such a step would, in my opinion, be unfortunate. After all, as multiple fan studies scholars have observed, fan texts are deeply enmeshed in their contextual environment and dialogic community structures (Booth 2010; Busse and Hellekson 2006). Educators can certainly provide this contextual information while teaching, but it is inevitable that the primary focus will remain on the exemplar under consideration. In addition, although potential ethical conflicts must always be kept in mind when considering how to incorporate fan works into pedagogical strategies, it is also vital that the nature of fan communities as dynamic and contested spaces be kept in mind.

To build on this point further I would argue that in academic work in the field, transformative fandom spaces are too often characterized as uniformly welcoming and harmonious in their functioning, particularly around the axes of gender and sexuality. Although it is certainly true that these communities are largely female and queer-identified, this does not mean that they are free from their own prejudices and biases, particularly around issues of racial identity. As I have noted in my examination of the changing dynamics of these communities (Pande 2016), these spaces have always had a heavy bias toward whiteness. And even though nonwhite fans have always articulated their discomfort with race and racism in fan spaces, the move to more dialogic platforms like Tumblr has boosted their critiques. This has taken various forms, such as directly critiquing the overwhelming popularity of white characters in fan works as a default or creating new forms of fan works that challenge the whitecentric popular media texts.

It was therefore a combination of both intracommunity dynamics and the actual fanwork exemplars produced within those debates that aided my own formulation of methodologies for teaching about race and racism in the context of popular culture in a whitecentric classroom. This is a particularly difficult scenario for educators to tackle, for the topic by its very nature introduces discomfort into the classroom. However, examining the ways in which this discomfort has been used creatively by nonwhite fans to interrupt the default whiteness of Hollywood casting choices enabled me to come up with a similar exercise for my students. In addition, evaluating the participatory nature of fandom spaces—wherein fans very often examine their own biases self-reflexively—gave me the tools to draw the students into demonstrating their own internalized assumptions instead of turning it into a purely theoretical, and therefore remote, exercise. Since these fan works, known popularly as racebending within fan communities, are not widely known outside them, I will now expand on them briefly before discussing the critical context of my own teaching assignment.

To put the rest of this chapter in context, I was teaching a second-year undergraduate unit for the course Reading Popular Culture (ENGL2801). The course was administered at the University of Western Australia's School of English and Cultural Studies. The course was aimed at introducing undergraduate students (from a variety of disciplines) to the practice of critically interpreting and interrogating popular culture.

INTERRUPTING THE DEFAULT: RACEBENDING AS RESISTANT FAN PRACTICE

Racebending has a complex history, both within and outside fandom. Commenting on this practice, Gaston and Reid (2012, 2.3) refer to Mica Pollack's formulation of it as "a strategy of questioning the validity of race categories to describe human diversity even while keeping race categories strategically available for the analysis of local and national racial inequalities." Within fandom, they observe, it refers to a casting choice in which a role with a particular racial identity (or ethnicity) ascribed to it is given to a performer not of that race or ethnicity without changing the actual script, or when a role's race or ethnicity is changed (reflected in scripting details) to match that of a chosen actor.

For Gaston and Reid (2012, 2.3), although this use of racebending may refer to a situation in which an actor of color performs an originally white character, "overwhelmingly, it has a more negative connotation wherein a character of color—indeed, often an actual person—has their race/ethnicity changed, and then that character/role is portrayed by a white actor (also contemporarily known as yellowface, for the still-acceptable practice—in contrast to blackface—of having white actors tape their eyes back or use makeup to portray Asians)."

It is certainly possible for the term *racebending* to be used both ways, but an observation of fandom practice seems to have shifted the term to the former definition, referring not just to official casting decisions but also to the practice in which fans come up with dream casts, or, in the case of texts already in film form, recasts so as to make them more diverse. A similar practice (often intersecting) is genderbending—that is, casting that puts more women into traditionally male roles in popular texts (Baker 2016). Whereas genderbending is a very popular practice within fan fiction, racebending is more common in visual media like fan art, and more particularly to the Tumblr platform, photosets, and gif-sets.

Gif-sets are made up of a file type called a gif (graphic interchange format) that allows for a few seconds of video footage to be looped indefinitely, facilitating an innovative new style of narrative in which fans poach footage from various sources to build stories. These can be in the form of credit montages that introduce various characters in their reimagined forms or can contain an exposition about the world building a particular reimagined universe in the form of a gif-fic. Commenting on their use, Perez (2013) observes that the gif-fic is a form of fan work that usually contains a symmetrical number of gifs so as to maximize the Tumblr format. She notes, "The number is enough to tell snippets of the story.... With a limited number of gifs, exposition and setup are often explained in an attached author's note or left to the reader's imaginations" (152).

This deliberate interruption and reformulation of what specific characters are supposed to look like is a very powerful tool for undercutting the default reading process in which a character is assumed to be white, even in the face of considerable textual evidence to the contrary. This is only reinforced when the descriptions of a character are more ambiguous. For instance, when the first film of the *Hunger Games* trilogy was made in 2012 and Amandla Stenberg was cast as the character of Rue, the reaction of some fans followed this logic of having assumed whiteness. These fans unleashed a barrage of tweets after their first viewing of the film that were shockingly vitriolic in terms of their racism.

For example, one user tweeted, "Awkward moment when Rue is some black girl and not the blonde innocent girl you picture" (D. Scott 2012). This particular sentiment—that an "innocent" young girl (as Rue is described in the text) *could* be played by a black actress—was a repeated refrain (Holmes 2012). In fact, Rue's description in the book suggests that she is unambiguously nonwhite. When Katniss Everdeen sees Rue for the first time, she describes her in the following terms: "And most hauntingly, a twelve-year-old girl from District 11. She has dark brown skin and eyes, but other than that she's very like Prim in size and demeanor" (Collins 2008, 45). The fact that so many fans of the books completely failed to take this very clear depiction into account shows how powerfully the assumption of whiteness operates in popular cultural texts.

This example also shows, once again, how the assumed subversiveness of fan spaces must never be left uninterrogated. The *Hunger Games* is, after all, a text that is led by a woman—although Katniss herself is also somewhat whitewashed in the films, compared to the book's description of her as having olive skin and straight black hair. Furthermore, its narrative emphasizes resistance to an oppressive social order. It could be assumed, therefore, that its fans would welcome more diversity in the supporting cast—that it would only build on the text's clear metaphors for institutionalized and racialized injustice (Heit 2015; Pharr et al. 2012). The fact that this did not happen, and that the appearance of Rue on screen caused such a degree of backlash, shows how deeply issues of race, especially blackness, still mediate such spaces.

It is in this context that I posit that the practice of racebending—in which characters (both those ambiguously described in textual form as well those who are canonically white) are deliberately rendered by fans in full and varying color—becomes a political act of resistance and a way of talking back to powerful discourses that coercively dictate what kinds of narratives in Western popular cultural texts are allowable for nonwhite characters. Although fan practices that inject queer sexualities into ostensibly straight texts have been central to examinations of media fan spaces from the inception of fan studies, there has been a ringing silence around other resistant practices. It should also be noted that racebending, in most cases, also takes into account other interstices of identity, including queer sexualities that are often erased in the most popular white character–centered pairings.

My own "aha" moment that connected this resistant fan practice with the possibilities of antiracist teaching came when I came across a gif-set that introduced a live-action remake of the 1999 Disney animated movie, *The Lion King* (stannisbarathenon, 2013), set in contemporary New York City. The gif-set imagined how the conflicts in the movie among family, ambition, betrayal, and love might play out with actors such as Idris Elba, Kerry Washington, and John Boyega playing lead roles. The reimagination made for powerful viewing because it forced the deracialized narrative of *The Lion King*—set in an undifferentiated "African" landscape with white actors such as Jeremy Irons (Scar), Matthew Broderick (Simba), and Rowan Atkinson (Zazu) doing the voice-overs for a majority of the characters—to be rerooted into material and visibly black bodies.

In addition, because of the popularity of the original text, the gif-set could depend on the narrative being recognized instantly and thus performed its critique in the space of just ten panels. The gif-set was also effective in reversing another strategy that is often used to justify the whitecentricity of mainstream Hollywood productions, whose creators have argued that such casting is necessary to reflect social reality. This is an argument deployed particularly regularly in the case of historical films—in which nonwhite characters are seen to be incongruous, if included at all—but it is also used to deflect criticism of the exclusion of these characters in science fiction and fantasy films as well. In the case of the *The Lion King* however, using the same metric, the gif-set argued implicitly that such casting was necessary to preserve the social realism of the narrative. Surely, if one were to imagine an accurate depiction of the story of the film, an all-black cast would be essential.

The effectiveness of the criticism mobilized by the fan remix sparked my critical imagination, and I began to consider how I could introduce its ethos into a classroom whose students were reading the theoretical material in the syllabus as a largely intellectual exercise, at a distance from their daily experiences. As I will expand on in the next section, creating an antiracist pedagogy is an extremely challenging task, rife with multiple possible pitfalls. I will now explore some of these in more detail in order to contextualize my specific methodology in creating the teaching assignment under discussion.

BREAKING THE SILENCE: ENABLING CRITICAL DISCUSSIONS ABOUT RACE AND RACISM IN THE CLASSROOM

It is no secret that to seek to spark a discussion about the effects of race and racism in any context is to tread on uncertain territory. Indeed, with the rise in right-wing conservatism in the global political sphere and the increasing neoliberal nature of college campuses, the challenges faced by educators who wish to challenge student perceptions about issues such as institutional racism, white privilege, and xenophobia will inevitably grow. In light of this it is therefore even more important for teachers to approach these issues equipped with the knowledge of critical race pedagogy as well as the willingness to explore the discomfort caused by these discussions.

I use the word *discomfort* repeatedly here to reference Boler's (1999) notion of a "pedagogy of discomfort." In her examination of student disaffection and distancing during the Persian Gulf War in the early 1990s, Boler found that repetitive media coverage of the event led to student disengagement, because they felt largely powerless to influence the world around them. It was only by reintroducing an affective element into classroom situations that led to students once again establishing a personal connection to seemingly overwhelming global issues. In light of this, Boler maintains, "Learning to live with ambiguity, discomfort, and uncertainty is a worthy educational ideal" (198).

This is especially relevant when considering college classrooms where white students form a majority; studies have repeatedly shown that conversations about race and racism in such setups are framed in either antagonistic terms or met with uncomfortable silence (Haltinner 2016; K. Martin 2010). This is also true for multicultural classrooms; discussions of race and racism can turn into hostile exchanges and an us-versus-them mentality. Although teachers sometimes seek to reduce this hostility by turning the exercise into a purely theoretical one, this may not be the most effective course if truly antiracist practices are to be attempted. Liston and Salim (2002) note the following:

> In the past I [Liston] tried to create a classroom that was caring and not acrimonious—one that was intellectually challenging but not personally discomforting. I now believe that I strove for an unrealistic and not very helpful ideal. I still strive to create a caring and supportive ethos, but I now also want to support and make safe the expression and reception of anger and frustration. I have come to believe that if white faculty and white students are going to examine issues of race and racism in the classroom, then conflict, struggle, and discomfort must be present. We need to learn how to express emotions and ideas, especially painful ones. (241)

Therefore, although in most cases it is important for educators to facilitate the creation of safe spaces in which to explore topics perceived as dangerous, we must also question what happens when it is necessary to introduce discomfort into the equation. How can students be encouraged to confront their own privilege in a way that engages them?

The question of engagement is also fraught with discomfort, and Gnanadass (2014) provides a useful example of how her strategy of immersive exercises toward this goal was not very successful. She describes how she used an activity called the Privilege Walk, adapted from McIntosh (1990). The activity required students (starting from the same place) to move forward if they benefited from a certain aspect of privilege associated with whiteness and backward if they did not. Their position at the end of the exercise was meant to bring home to them the nature of their individual levels of privilege in an institutional context. She recalls, however, that the exercise ended up prompting anger and shame in the students who moved to the front of the class and hopelessness and frustration in the ones who moved backward. She also observed, "The body language, the whispered conversations in a usually boisterous and interactive class, and the journal entries on this activity indicated students' resentment and misunderstanding about privilege, especially the structural nature of White privilege. I also did not deal with it well, because I was uncomfortable confronting and talking about students' guilt and discomfort with White privilege myself. I was able to intellectually examine Whiteness as overdetermined by race, class, gender, and nationality, but was not able to discuss it constructively to help students think through the structural aspects of Whiteness and race in the U.S. context" (98).

Both Liston and Salim and Gnanadass therefore point to possible shortcomings in these two different approaches toward creating an antiracist pedagogical practice. While for Liston the inadequacy revolved around a disengagement from discomfort, for Gnanadass the introduction of discomfort did not enable any constructive outcomes. For me, the question around which a possible third approach oscillated was complex: How could I inject a livedness and interactive element into discussions of race and racism while also not imposing a definition of privilege through a checklist? In my opinion, Gnanadass's initial strategy faltered when certain students were blocked into acknowledging positions of privilege in a way that did not implicate their own decisions and so led to feelings of shame and anger.

It was with these objectives in mind that I turned toward racebending, particularly the gif-set referenced earlier, in order to create an assignment that implicated the students in a decision-making process that would exemplify their own inherent biases. In the case of fandom, racebent gif-sets and art can provide a means of introducing both conflict and discomfort into seemingly harmonious and liberal spaces. On one level, these fan works introduce conflict while interfacing with the source text itself, showing how familiar narratives can be expanded to encompass brand new imaginative spaces with surprising actors in their lead roles. On another level, they confront fellow fans on their easy acceptance, consumption, and elevation of whitecentric casts through fan work that does not question their popularity. The ways in which white fans in particular react to such confrontations are, of course, varied, but their attention is certainly always already engaged because of their familiarity with the source narratives. This can have the effect of drawing them into newer forms of interfacing with issues of race and racism within both media texts and fandom spaces and perhaps seeing how so-called universal narratives are almost always enacted by white people. I will now discuss how I incorporated these aspects of fandom discomfort in my methodology as I developed the assignment in more detail.

ASSIGNMENT METHODOLOGY

The assignment under discussion was designed for a course called Reading Popular Culture (ENGL2801), a second-year unit at the University of Western Australia's School of English and Cultural Studies. The unit was concerned with introducing students to a range of issues and readings stemming from different disciplines but all concerned with a broader attempt to read popular culture through a critical lens. The unit focused on certain key theorists who have been influential in cultural studies and drew its readings from various key schools of cultural criticism such as Marxism, postmodernism, and feminism. Through an in-depth reading of these theorists, students were encouraged to gain critical literacy in theoretical movements as well as to examine how all their cultural practices—from visiting museums to Googling the latest meme—reveal how they read the world continuously and make meaning from it.

The structure of the class was divided into a weekly one-hour lecture and two-hour tutorial. The assignment under discussion was administered in the tenth week of the unit and had to work in concert with the larger assigned readings that week, which were taken up in the main lecture. These assigned readings were concerned with historical and theoretical considerations of how race, racism, and white privilege affect popular cultural texts. The assigned readings were comprehensive and relevant, but it was observed that students were operating with somewhat of a disconnection to the relationship between theory and everyday practice. The assignment was therefore concerned with making the theory more immediately relevant to the students' contemporary lives.

As I have already discussed, the need to develop an antiracist pedagogy was foremost in my mind. However, I was also concerned with helping my students, many of whom had expressed interest in pursuing further research, to develop a sense of theoretical literacy. That is, I wanted to show them that critical theory was not just something abstract or confined to a university setting but rather something that had a material connection with their living realities. Furthermore, within a neoliberal university structure, where a more use-based model of education is favored, it is sometimes perceived that a humanities education has no real-life applications. I wished to combat this assertion by designing an assignment that encouraged students to apply the theoretical lens they were studying to a popular cultural context that would have an immediate impact on their conceptual frameworks. Dale's (1969) focus on the effectiveness of experiential learning was also formative in my design process.

It was also important for me to ground my methodology in specifically antiracist strategies and go beyond the lip-service often paid to such issues. Biren, Gurin, and Lopez (2003, 166) observed, "Simply having diverse campuses does not automatically lead to direct effects on learning outcomes. ... Colleges and universities must use that diversity to create learning opportunities in classrooms and in the broader campus environment for students to learn from each other." Their approach to achieving such opportunities melded Freire's (1970) dialogic model of education with Kolb's (1984) theory of experiential learning. They stressed three factors—content, an active learning pedagogy, and engaged learning—and elaborated on them in the following manner:

> In terms of content, all the streams emphasize a structural analysis of oppression and inclusion of marginalized voices.
>
> In terms of pedagogy, Freire's dialogic process—encouraging collective inquiry into social reality—corresponds to the reflective learning in Kolb's model and to the participatory learning that is emphasized in multicultural education. Active learning is seen to be critical. Education must encourage students to become active inquirers and transformers of the world around them.
>
> In terms of engaged learning, the three streams also converge in expanding the boundaries of the learning environment from inside the classroom to include students' outside-the-classroom experiences. (Biren et al. 2003, 169–70)

There is a great deal of synergy between these principles and the fan practices that I have discussed so far. First, in terms of content, although the popular cultural texts that are the base of fan works are often disappointingly lacking in diverse casting or story lines, by racebending those narratives, fans can enable an imaginative extension that defies that erasure. Second, as I have already pointed out, racebending as a resistant fan work arose out of the dialogic nature of fan spaces, especially as they have moved toward platforms that allow for greater visibility of critique. Third, the participatory nature of fan communities means that engagement in these debates is a matter of course. These three streams were also reflected in the structure of the assignment, as I will now detail further.

ASSIGNMENT STRUCTURE AND WORKING

Because I hoped to incorporate the assignment into a larger preset course structure, I decided not to overload the students with too much extra reading material. In any case, since the lecture had already gone through the critical theory quite exhaustively, I was more interested in bringing that material into a more engaged mode of learning. The assignment consisted of a prereading, a link to a short video, and an exercise, along with some discussion questions that the students were instructed to think about before the tutorial. The assignment was e-mailed to the students three days before the tutorial.

The assignment components were as follows:

- The reading was a short essay. Like Gnanadass, I too used "White Privilege: Unpacking the Invisible Knapsack" by Peggy McIntosh (1990).
- A short video was linked in which filmmaker Nelson George (2011) critiqued the movie *The Help*. Even though it was a critically acclaimed film, Nelson explained that it suffers from the same problems that have plagued Hollywood's depiction of the civil rights movement in America—particularly between 1958 and 1965, like *Mississippi Burning* (1988) and *A Time To Kill* (1996). These narratives perpetually frame the struggle for civil rights as a struggle in the past, thus signaling that those rights have been won. Furthermore, these movies are always framed from the point of view of a white character, which has the effect of once again recentering whiteness. Students were asked to bring short responses to questions about the video to be taken up further in group discussions.
- The students were asked to imagine themselves as directors, making a live-action adaptation of the movie *The Lion King*. As discussed earlier, I wished to find out what default reading positions the students would bring to an intimately familiar text that was at once marked and unmarked by racial signifiers. The object of the casting process was to observe which real-life Hollywood actors would be cast for these roles. Would the students racebend the cast themselves, having been primed throughout the exercise to look for structural inequalities in Hollywood, or would the theoretical concepts we had been discussing remain remote?

The design of the assignment therefore followed Biren et al.'s (2003) model—content, dialogic activity, and participatory learning—to encourage students to move from theory to practice, from passive to engaged modes of learning. The proposed learning outcomes of the assignment, consequently, were to understand and critically engage with the notions of white privilege and racial power relations in popular culture; engage in discussion about race and representation in contemporary Hollywood films; link theoretical discussion with real-world experiences to see the effects of those relations; and exchange ideas in a group discussion format.

The students were responsive to the instructions of the assignment and came to the class having read the material and watched the short video. I also played the video again and asked them to engage with the material in the context of the group discussion questions. The tutorial went quite smoothly, almost too smoothly, as students nodded along with the points made in the McIntosh essay and also expressed disapproval at Hollywood's racist casting practices and problematic framing of civil rights issues as analyzed by Nelson George. I had expected some resistance on the issue of white privilege, but the students broadly agreed on the validity of the concept and its influence on societal structures.

I could see, however, that the problem of race and racism in popular culture was still on the outside, practiced by other people. When we got to the casting exercise, things suddenly got a whole lot more engaged. As I asked for casting suggestions and wrote them down on the whiteboard, it became increasingly obvious that the majority of the names suggested were of white actors. In fact, out of the twenty-eight actors proposed, only *four* were non-white, and only one, Donald Glover, was black. Although this fact was glaring to me, it did not seem to impinge on the consciousness of the class, *despite* the subject matter we had so rigorously been discussing. This served to underline once again how powerfully whiteness as the default operates in our consciousness. Once the nominations were over, I stood back and finally asked, "Why are there were so many white actors in a story very clearly set somewhere in Africa?"

There was a moment of silence as the students suddenly realized that they had just reenacted the very racist casting practices they had spent the last hour critiquing. Race and racism in popular culture was instantly transposed from something done by people in Hollywood to something actively engineered by the students themselves. The rest of that class was not smooth at all; it produced an extremely engaged debate as students confronted their own biases. The students had so far been rather quiet, but they suddenly became a lot more vocal in arguing the fact that the exercise was a direct product of their own prejudice. One student said quite heatedly, "There are white people in Africa, too, you know!" I agreed, and then pushed her to justify why this specific narrative—that of a royal family that seemingly drew from indigenous customs and languages—should be enacted by white people. This rhetorical reversal—having to justify the presence of whiteness instead of defending the inclusion of blackness—had a powerful effect on both the individual student and the class as a whole.

In effect, what had been an academic and intellectual discussion was now reframed in immediate terms and prompted a wide range of energized and engaged responses. Some students questioned the casting exercise itself, seeking to excuse their biases by pointing to the influence of the original voice-over actors on their decisions. Others reiterated the ever popular argument of there not being enough nonwhite actors to choose from. At this point I reminded them of the discussions we had just had debunking these very assumptions. In this way the students were asked once more to contemplate their complicity in the structural influences that had, so far, seemed to be far outside their influence.

The students therefore engaged in all three modes of transformative learning outlined by Biren et al. (2003) by debating the structural oppressions in the world around them in a participatory manner and acknowledging their own implicit biases. By tracking the discussion, I observed that the issues that had been so far discussed as "out there" or as the fault of a generalized notion of big-budget movie producers were suddenly and forcefully brought home to the students: they had been put in charge of a creative process and had reproduced the same oppressive conditions. It was a confrontational method, but it encouraged them to participate in a deeper mode of engagement.

RESULTS AND REFLECTIONS

The module demonstrated that a practice-based antiracist pedagogy definitely has a place within the discipline of the humanities. The students' level of engagement with the theory was in fact heightened when a more hands-on approach was taken. The students were also clear in their approval of structured tasks with identifiable outcomes. Although it is in the nature of the discipline (and in fact one of its advantages) to be open-ended and encouraging of original thought, giving students some more structure in their tutorials could be advantageous to these objectives. Students who initially struggled with discipline expectations were seen to respond well when the assignment set out clear objectives and expectations. This did not limit discussion but had the effect of streamlining it. Although the class was of a small sample size, the results certainly have implications for the ways in which traditional tutorials are structured in English and cultural studies. The efficacy of the teaching and learning strategies enumerated in the methodology section was supported by the findings.

Furthermore, I speculate that the actual content of the issues engaged with will lead students to be more aware of the structural inequalities around them, as reflected in numerous popular cultural texts and industries. This is not something that can be measured, of course, but student responses certainly indicate that a deeper mode of engagement did result. Finally, to reflect once again on the efficacy of a "pedagogy of discomfort," I was certainly aware of a rise of tension and confrontational attitudes in the students. However, the emotions were not shame or anger but rather shock and surprise. By implicating them in a demonstrably racist exercise but allowing their own actions to dictate their involvement, the assignment was successful in engaging students in difficult discussions in a way that had an impact without alienating them.

Did everyone walk out of that class feeling comfortable? I would say no. But I think that the discomfort was productive. Fan communities often get disturbed when nonwhite fans begin to point out the biases in a beloved text or indeed in fannish practices themselves. These are frequently very tense debates, because white fans—who often also experience marginalization because of their gender or their sexuality—seek to displace the causes of racism in these communities onto larger societal structures. As I have argued in my work on these communities in other contexts (Pande 2016), it is vital to see this displacement as an effect of the structuring force of whiteness even within ostensibly liberal spaces. However, at the same time it is also productive to examine the ways in which nonwhite fans attempt to interrupt the operations of this structuring force and raise awareness about its effects. I would argue, therefore, that it is the introduction of disturbance and discomfort into fandom communities that has provided the impetus for the production of innovative forms of fan work like racebending. As I have demonstrated, these practices not only offer new forms of critique, engagement, and debate within fandom spaces but can also point toward equally innovative ways for educators to confront the issues of race and racism in the classroom.

ANALYSIS OF STUDENT RESPONSES

Apart from my own observations, feedback from the students was collected to evaluate their perceptions of the assignment. Fifteen students were surveyed directly after the class. In order to get their honest opinions, I kept their responses anonymous. They were asked for some structural feedback on the assignment—whether the connections between the themes of the unit and the exercise were clear and if there had been enough time to engage with the prereading and video—as well as their feelings about the casting exercise and how it affected their engagement with the theory we had been discussing throughout the week.

In terms of structural comments, the students all responded positively to the assignment and approved of the supplementary materials. All of them agreed that it provided them with an active, engaged, and original way of interacting with the unit material and prompted useful discussion on the topic in a way that had not been facilitated so far by the regular lecture and tutorial structure. One student noted, "I liked this module as it gave me a clear outline of what to prepare, what to consider, and how the theory can be applied. I would enjoy more tutes [tutorials] being structured this way, especially if readings from the textbook could be integrated." The supplementary material was also appreciated, with one student commenting, "Yes [I like the additional material]. More active learning. I liked this reading more than the actual textbooks."

When the students were queried about the effect of the racebending recasting exercise, the responses were again extremely animated. Some students reflected on how the class had gone from a largely intellectualized discussion of theoretical concepts to an active interrogation of real-world dynamics. This was clearly a novel experience for the class, even though it was a response I had been attempting to encourage through different strategies each week. My success in animating the discussion in this case was registered in repeated student reflections on it being "loud." One student noted this change in dynamics: "The heated response in class evidenced this [newer ways of engagement with material]."

The students also seemed eager to repeat the more interactive aspect of the casting exercise, noting that they appreciated the ways in which it made them reevaluate the theoretical readings they had done that week. One student observed, "Even though we had been talking about racism in Hollywood all week, the casting exercise was still quite surprising. I hadn't thought about the movie in that way before." These responses are indicative of the fact that the assignment did work as I had hoped, with racebending prompting students to ground their evaluations of the film in more direct and material ways. Repeating the emphasis on discussions being prompted, yet another student commented, "More Lion King exercises. They were fun and encouraged discussion."

Although some students inevitably did react negatively to the assignment in their assessments—repeating complaints that the instructions on the casting exercise weren't clear enough—overall the class remains one of the most engaged, energized, and challenging tutorials I have conducted in that unit. There were no negative reactions to the debate itself, perhaps because the time allotted to the discussion was more circumscribed than is the case with discussions on racebending in fandom spaces. To explore this aspect, it would be interesting to track how these exercises could be incorporated earlier in a teaching session in order to allow more time for debate. In addition, within fandom spaces it is often the case that multiple racebent fan works critique one another as well the source texts—often taking up issues such as colorism, in which fair-skinned actors of color are routinely cast more than darker-skinned ones, even by fans creating resistant fanwork. It would perhaps be a productive addendum to use multiple exercises over a number of classes to further explore intersections of identity and so push the discussion to have even more nuance.

Finally, although the demands of the neoliberal university requires educators to be wary of negative student engagement and feedback, in this case I was glad to receive some evidence of the discomfort that the exercise had prompted, because that was also (ironically, perhaps) a rubric of success in this case. I hope that this reflection will be useful to other educators who wish to push their antiracist pedagogy in new and innovative directions, taking advantage of the lessons we can learn from creative and resistant fan practices.

WAVES OF FANDOM IN THE FAN STUDIES CLASSROOM

Paul Booth

On the first day of my Fandom and Active Audience classes (both the graduate version and the undergraduate), students come together who may never have met. To try to break through this unfamiliarity, I use the classic icebreaker: "What are you a fan of?" The answers, as we might expect, vary considerably. For some students, talking about fandom is a fairly difficult activity. Geraghty (2012, 170) argues, the "invisible fandom" of university students means they "do not see themselves in the very texts they study; . . . [they] are also unaware, or at least unwilling to recognize, the fact that the media pervades our lives so much that we all act as fans now." Students may not see themselves as fans. These students will, however almost invariably (and with only a modicum of coaching from myself) admit that they really love some sports team or some type of product—usually Apple. Other students are far more open about their fannish experiences: some will go far beyond what I ask and detail not only *what* they are fans of but also the *types* of fan activities they engage in (e.g., "I write fan fiction and read Tumblr and make GIFs for *Doctor Who*"). Others may find that fandom is difficult to talk about, because everyone practices their fandom—and fan identities—differently.

Of course, not every student considers themself a fan. Just loving the Apple brand doesn't necessarily make one a fan. But bringing together students with different backgrounds, experiences, and expectations of fandom and fan audiences is one of the primary challenges of teaching the fan studies class. Fandom has become so pervasive in contemporary students' lives that many of the activities that students do in their everyday lives have antecedents in, or are versions of, practices that fans have done for decades. Students (like fans) post GIFs and memes on Tumblr; they talk about and critique the media texts they love; they attend conventions and form social groups centered on their favorite texts. Although they might not call themselves fans (but many do), the activities they engage in are fannish in nature.

Although not all students may consider themselves fans, I believe that the fan studies classroom is a good opportunity for students to make connections between their own experience of the media today and the historical situation of fandom in the past fifty years (see appendix B). Whether or not students self-identify as fans, it's important for them to recognize the place of fandom in the media environment and the way that fandom has become more visible and more mainstream today. As I demonstrate in the class (and in this chapter), I attempt to do this by having students produce fan work.

In contrast to a course like the history of cinema, where at least the instructor can be reasonably sure that the students have, at one time or another, seen a film, a fan studies course must introduce the concept of fandom to students who may never have thought critically about whether they are fans or who have only stereotypical notions of fandom. However, Geraghty (2012, 163), in a useful chapter about the challenges of teaching fan studies to university students, notes that "those students who are wary of studying fandom and see themselves as separate from it are ultimately as much a part of participatory culture as any diehard fan. In other words, even if students don't see themselves as part of fan culture, in today's highly mediated and digital environment, they are exposed to fandom and engage in activities that reflect aspects of fan culture" (Gray et al., 2007, 7).

In this chapter I examine how the waves of fan studies (as described by Gray et al. 2007; see also Booth 2013) can be used as a heuristic in the fan studies classroom. As fandom becomes more normalized in popular culture—or, at least, the act of being a fan becomes more common—the tenor of class discussion about fandom shifts as well. I have previously written (Booth 2012) about some of the ethical dimensions of using fan activities in the classroom, but in this chapter I want to offer, first, a scholarly focus on what the methodological import of fan studies can tell us about teaching fans and teaching fandom. I argue that teaching fan studies can benefit from utilizing historical aspects of the waves as complementary to students' own media experiences and from viewing fan studies itself as an object worthy of study.

Second, and related to the first point, I explore a pedagogy of fan studies to examine the integration of fan voices into the fan studies classroom. By focusing on what I have previously called the "fourth wave" of fan studies (Booth 2013), or a turn to the "meta" in fan studies, I argue that students can find their own space in the fan community. In other words, I frame fan studies as both a discipline and an object of study, and I demonstrate this in the classroom by bringing fans in as guest speakers and to act as exemplars. This perspective offers a pedagogical viewpoint of fan studies. The fan studies instructor can enable student appreciation of the fan at the center of fan studies along with student identification of fan practices in their future lives after they graduate.

But how do we convince students—or, rather, teach them—about this ubiquity? In my classroom I have found that the best way to do this is through a two-tiered approach. First, I focus on the historical development of fan studies and fan texts. Fan studies as a discipline has shifted its focus over time. Perhaps this is unsurprising, since fan studies has now been around longer than a lot of the texts and the fans it is used to investigate. According to Gray, Harrington, and Sandvoss (2007), fan studies has gone through three of these shifts: the first wave of ethnographic research, the second wave of cultural studies, and the third wave of everyday fandom, or fan studies' "fundamental insights into modern life" (9). These waves of fan studies have culminated, at least according to these researchers, by "studying fan audiences ... to explore some of the key mechanisms through which we interact with the mediated world at the heart of our social, political, and cultural realities and identities" (10).

The third wave of fan studies, therefore, can be used as a heuristic for examining the way life is lived today, and applying this in the classroom means focusing on the various ways that fans and fandom have affected our media life (Deuze 2012). I have argued that fan studies has entered a fourth wave, one of meta-analysis, or exploration of fan studies itself (Booth 2013). And, indeed, scholars like Bennett (2014), Hills (2014a, 2014b), Ford (2014), and Coppa (2014) have all examined how fan studies scholars are becoming more introspective and more determined to uncover the effect of fan studies in the twenty-first century.

Therefore, my first tier of teaching focuses on the historical development of fan studies, tying it directly to the experiences of the students. Although Geraghty (2012, 164) finds that the students in his classes are hesitant to self-identify as fans and "do not see themselves as passionate about their activities as perhaps those who dress up in their favourite *Star Trek* costume or watch all episodes of 24 season eight on DVD back to back in one day," I have not found this to be the case. Rather, I have found that students become engaged in the lessons when they can see the historical precedent for their own activities and enthusiasm. Although some students self-select into my fan studies class (i.e., they sign up for a class on fandom because they self-identify as fans), many more of my students do not self-identify as fans.

The challenge and the opportunity of the fan studies classroom is to integrate both groups' engagement. This engagement is, I argue, a pedagogical necessity for the fan studies classroom.

To engage students more openly with fandom, I not only encourage them on the first day, through the icebreaker, to state their fan identities, I also give them a termlong assignment that asks them to analyze their fandom as it applies to their own lives. The second tier of my two-tiered approach, therefore, is to engage students in their own fandom by requiring them to explore the cult aspects of their favorite media text, write fan fiction about that text, explore in depth the fan community of that text, and make a fan video and summarize its relationship to the community. Even if they do not self-identify as fans, by working in the same vein as fans do, the students emulate a fan experience and make connections to their own experiences. Similarly, Geraghty (2012) finds a more positive reaction in teaching a fan fiction creative writing course: students meet the task "with tremendous enthusiasm" (165). Thus, by integrating both academic and fannish voices into the curriculum, students see the fan in the acafan and the scholar in the scholar-fan (Hills 2002; Zubernis and Larsen 2012).

TIER ONE: FAN STUDIES AND THE WAVES OF FANDOM

My two fan classes are geared toward the historical development of fan studies as a field and tying that field directly to the experiences of the students. In terms of the historical development of fan studies, the class is focused on developing a working competency of the past twenty-five years of scholarship about fans. The relatively brief history of fan studies as a discipline makes it ideally suited to teaching in a quarter or a semester; students can be introduced to the field through introductory readings, be taken back to the beginning of the field with more classic readings, and then be at the cutting edge of contemporary fan studies research. This includes the new work coming out in *Transformative Works and Cultures* and the *Journal of Fandom Studies* as well as the many new books on fandom published in recent years. In contrast to something like English literature, or even film studies, which has a much longer history, the breadth and expanse of fan studies can fit neatly into one course (with the caveat that it is possible to investigate these concepts even further in more specific classes).

There is a big difference between teaching *fans* and teaching *fan studies*; it is how I differentiate teaching my undergraduate course, Fandom and Participatory Cultures, and my graduate course, Fandom and Active Audiences. In the undergraduate course, students *become transformative fans*: they experience what it is like to write fan fiction, to make fan videos, to seek out beta readers, and to discuss with critical intent some of their most sacred texts (Jenkins 1992). Students appreciate this approach—my course evaluations often feature comments like "It stimulated my creativity while enabling me to think critically" or "The way the course is set up was incredibly helpful to my understanding of the topic at hand." My graduate students do these activities as well, but they take a more self-critical, autoethnographic approach, which, as one student commented, helps "introduce [them] to a whole new field of study in fan studies that [they did] not realize was a concentration prior to this class." This type of scholar-fandom asks the students to look specifically at their own fan identities as a product of a specific culture, social situation, and history (Hills 2002, 3).

According to Bennett (2014), "the position of the scholar-fan, or aca-fan, where the researcher is simultaneously an academic and fan has been introduced and understood as a dual role that, although liminal, can offer complicated advantages from both perspectives" (11). Indeed, Bennett mentions that the history of scholar-fandom goes back to Jenkins's (1992) canonical work on fan studies: "I write both as an academic (who has access to certain theories of popular culture, certain bodies of critical and ethnographic literature) and as a fan (who has access to the particular knowledge and traditions of that community)" (Bennett, 2014, 5–6). The best practices that I have found pedagogically in teaching the history of the discipline come in two forms. First, the selection of readings I choose implicitly asks students to compare and contrast the early days of fan studies to contemporary fan studies scholarship. Second, in my teaching I explicitly bring up and discuss the different waves of fan scholarship. Students respond well to this focus; one recently wrote on a course evaluation that the class "got me to think critically about fans and fandom, and not just take things [at] 'face value.'"

I've previously described how fandom can be used to discuss ethical issues in the classroom (Booth 2012). I ask students to compare and contrast classic readings (which, although only a few decades old, appear ancient to students born at the cusp of the twenty-first century) with contemporary ones. For example, when discussing the history of fandom, I have students contrast the first chapter of Jenkins (1992) (and we watch William Shatner's infamous

1986 "Get a Life!" sketch from *Saturday Night Live*), marking the start of fan studies, with Bennett (2014), which highlights the contributions the work and fan studies have made over the past twenty-five years, and Busse's (2013) discussion of hierarchies in fan audiences.

In a later class we discuss the performative aspects of fandom, exploring this in Lancaster (2001) and in Geraghty (2014). Both books offer unique and valuable insights into the nature of fannish performance—Lancaster in terms of the performance studies paradigm, which views fans as actively constructive of their own identities, and Geraghty in terms of the concrete and tangible elements of the performance of fandom through paratextual objects (see also Booth 2015b). Though separated by only thirteen years, the books span a vast time frame for students approaching fan studies for the first time.

The result of this implicit contrast of readings is that students encounter both the evolution of thought in the discipline, which affects their own critical faculties, and critical works that speak to one another. Noting the moments when Jenkins (1992), for instance, offers a more utopian view of fan activity whereas Busse (2013) argues the more hierarchical view gives students a critical eye. The implicit contrasts between different fan studies viewpoints allows the students to read each as making particular arguments that do not necessarily have a right or a wrong answer but only reflect different argumentation strategies. Reading articles focused on similar topics against each other allows students to see multiple viewpoints rather than get a top-down notion of what fandom is. In this way the fan studies classroom allows a greater emphasis on the nature of fandom itself—an exploration of different viewpoints and ideas all centered on a particular text. Pedagogically, this creates a safe space, a classroom in which alternate viewpoints are not only expressed but encouraged, and students see different ideas expressed in the writing, which influences their own expression of ideas.

I offer the metaphor of the waves of fandom, as according to Gray, Harrington, and Sandvoss (2007), as a way of exploring the connections between fandom and fan studies over time. As noted above, the first wave of fan studies, as Jenkins (1992, 86) puts it, saw fandom as "an institution of theory and criticism, a semistructured space where competing interpretations and evaluations of common texts are proposed, debated, and negotiated and where readers speculate about the nature of the mass media and their own relationship to it."

In other words, the first wave dealt with fans as a collective and made fan activity more visible (Booth 2013). When discussing the first wave, I usually introduce students to the concept of slash fiction. According to Geraghty (2012, 166), "the most extreme reaction comes when students are introduced to Slash Fiction," and I have found this to be true as well. Initially, some students embrace the idea that, as Jenkins (1992, 189) writes, "slash fiction represents a reaction against the construction of male sexuality on television and ... invites us to imagine something akin to the liberating transgression of gender hierarchy," but others are more resistant, feeling as though any fiction that takes *that* sort of liberty with the text is not only incorrect, it's also damaging to the media environment. Many students are particularly resistant to this reading, especially when finding their own fan object under scrutiny. Geraghty (2012, 166) notes that this partly stems from "the fact that this [fan studies] scholarship and knowledge includes being familiar with communities, fan practices and those media texts a typical student might ordinarily avoid." Students don't want to question what they feel as part of *their* environment: fandom is popular media, after all. When students pose this in a framework of first-wave fandom, however, they are able to separate their personal feelings for or against slash and see it as an aspect of fan history within fan studies. Historical placement reframes the discourse.

Reframing this discourse initially allows students to reapproach slash as a contemporary genre of fan fiction when we discuss it toward the end of class. I reintroduce slash when we examine social justice and fandom and when we look at digital fan practices. As a comment on issues of gender representation in the media and as a larger sociopolitical reaction to cultural perceptions of normative heterosexual gender norms, slash confronts students' own perceptions. By *initially* framing it as historical and *then* introducing it again in a more contemporary setting, I use the waves of fan studies to try to offset students' initial resistance.

The second wave of fan studies deals with the "replication of social and cultural hierarchies within fan- and subculture ... as a reflection and further manifestation of our social, cultural, and economic capital" (Gray et al. 2007, 6). In class this manifests as an exploration of different ways of interpreting value within fan communities (Jenkins, Ford, and Green 2013, 85–113). We explore the gift economy (De Kosnik 2009; Hellekson 2009), the "regift" economy (S. Scott 2009), the "Digi-gratis" economy (Booth 2010), and the commercial economy of the Web (Terranova 2003; Geraghty 2014). The contrasts between the different types of economies become more clear as class continues, and the students become more comfortable sharing their own personal fandoms in class. Pedagogically, this opens up the classroom for a more free-flowing discussion of ideas; in short, the classroom itself becomes a type of gift economy as the students share their own stories of their fandom. Students necessarily practice their fandom in different ways, and by externalizing the discussion of how fan practices emerged in the past, the students are able to contextualize their own fannish practices today.

The third wave of fan studies departs from the first two. Instead of examining fandom in and of itself, it uses fandom "as a part of the fabric of our everyday lives" to "capture fundamental insights into modern life" (Gray et al. 2007, 9). One of the ways fan scholars can initiate this type of analysis is by examining the representation of fans in mainstream media. By critically evaluating the development of the representation from the early days of fan studies (e.g., Shatner's sketch) to more contemporary representations, like the fans of the TV series *The Big Bang Theory*, students can learn about these "fundamental insights into modern life." In other words, what do representations of fans teach us about contemporary media audiences?

Students in my class watch the film *Trekkies* and react to the positive and negative representations in it. We discuss more recent representations of fans, including *The Big Bang Theory* and the film *Fanboys*. We return to slash fiction, often in the guise of *Supernatural* Wincest fiction (slash fiction about the brothers Winchester), and open up to the way that slash fiction is referenced in popular culture today (like *Supernatural*, which openly discusses it; see Schmidt 2010). Students process the different representations as not just existent but also as *constructed with a particular discourse*. They see why some fans are mocked whereas others are extolled. I've called this the "hyperfan" discourse of fan representation: one overt representation is pitted against a more normative fan in order to discipline fan audiences (Booth 2015c). Through these examinations, students see how, for instance, the fans that are extolled in these videos are often the ones complicit with the media industries, the ones who celebrate the text rather than transform it. Students see how fans with transgressive undertones are disciplined in order to develop more acceptable images of fandom today. They understand insights into the contemporary media world.

In the course of teaching the class, however, I've harnessed my students' own fan voices to help cohere the waves of fandom into an interconnected understanding of contemporary fandom. For instance, each student in my class writes a piece of fan fiction and makes a fan video for a self-selected media text. This allows the students to see the work that goes into a particular aspect of fandom and allows them to understand the fan experience from the fannish side. In the next section I explore how my students' autoethnographies, when coupled with the use of fans' own voices, turns the classroom into an affinity space of shared meaning.

TIER TWO: INTEGRATING FANNISH VOICES

When my students engage in creating their own fan texts, I ask them to question their own relationship to fan studies. This critical questioning is, I would argue, a fourth wave of fan studies, in which there has been a turn from analyzing fans to analyzing fan studies. The students in my fan class personify this transition. Since they do not see themselves as the types of fans in any of the previous waves, students' self-perception is of their unique place in the media environment. My classroom attempts to situate students historically within similar fan practices. Similar to Geraghty (2012, 165), I find that "when students start to research their creative practices they shy away from a critical engagement with fan scholarship and offer a largely surface analysis of what they wrote and why they chose a particular media text to write about." This is perhaps because of the topics I choose to teach about: slash fiction is a fascinating topic, and students love to discuss their reactions (both positive and negative) to slash as well as engage in debates about the rationale behind fans' writing of slash. But very few students write slash fiction for their fan fiction assignment.

Students see themselves in a different relationship to fandom, especially today, when many of the activities they engage in on a daily basis—posting to Tumblr, tweeting to celebrities, making GIFs—might be considered fannish by fan scholars but not by students (Booth 2015c; Bennett and Chin 2014). Does the discursive identification of fandom by fan studies hail fandom into being (Booth 2015c, 150–72)? Or, to put this in terms of my classroom, do I hail my students as fans even if they do not?

Ultimately, the methodological issue here raises much larger questions about the discursive nature of academic study, questions that we can approach in class as students begin their autoethnographic investigation. Indeed, Hills (2002, 51) writes that "autoethnography must constantly seek to unsettle the use of theory as a disguise for personal attachments and investments." Students may write fan fiction but rarely call it that; more often they're discussing their fandom with their friends or "geeking out" over the latest episode of *Game of Thrones*. As Hills (2014a, 32) notes, "Fan writings that are neither textual exegesis nor fiction have generally been under-researched and under-theorized." Asking students in class to *become* fans by constructing a particular type of fan text—fan fiction and fan videos—may seem a strict interpretation of what fandom actually is, but it gives credence to the *discipline* of fan studies by supporting and connecting the pathways of the waves discussed by Gray, Harrington, and Sandvoss (2007). Indeed, by (in effect) forcing students to engage in a process of writing fan fiction that fans have been doing for centuries (Jamison 2013) and making fan videos, which fans have been doing for at least forty years (Coppa 2008), I take students on the historical journey of fans and allow them to reinscribe their own place in fan history. As one student wrote, the class takes "things that you just take for granted, like fan fiction, and [shows] you how you can view them critically and understand how they affect the greater picture in culture." (It is relevant here that this student takes fan fiction for granted; it is a natural part of students' lives today.)

I bring examples to class of fan work from the past, including fan fiction we read in class and fan videos we analyze. This method is not without its ethical dimensions: using fan work without the creator's permission might be seen as a violation of privacy or as an intrusion into fannish space. I try to only use works that have been deliberately archived and posted on websites by groups like the Organization for Transformative Works or on the fans' own websites. From a historical perspective, looking at work that the readings cite helps to contextualize the students' own experiences with the fan text.

Fandom is, in many ways, a participatory culture (Jenkins 2006c), and by creating a space in which students can create fan work and share fan work—because we have been exploring fan work from the start of the class—the classroom moves from a space of membership (all are in the class because they signed up) to a space of interaction (students learn from one another and from their own experiences). Although my classroom is not a voluntary fan community (e.g., one formed by groups of people bonded over a similar text), it is a community of students who volunteered to study fandom; the course is not required for graduation nor does it fulfill a general education requirement. Students sign up for the class because they are interested in the material, and as the instructor I play off this interest.

Gee (2005) has termed this type of classroom an "affinity space," in which learning happens through small-group work, student-teacher interactions, and peer contributions. In addition to utilizing lecture and the explication of facts, affinity-space learning encourages students to critically engage in their own interests. Affinity-space learning turns the classroom into a space of intense student engagement, facilitated by an instructor, where "safely controlled and monitored transgressions may in fact blossom into a greater understanding and respect for the very norms being transgressed" (Booth 2012, 184). The affinity space of the fan studies classroom allows students to engage in fan work that might challenge, and therefore develop, their historical and contemporary perceptions of their own level of fannishness.

In addition to providing a space for students to voice their own particular fandom, I open up the classroom to other fan voices as well. Fandom is more than just a subject to study; it is a number of actual, living communities, each with its own mores. Studying fandom means listening to fans; as a 2015 fan studies course at the University of California at Berkeley demonstrated, when students were asked to enter fan communities without recognition of these traditions, the fans became alienated rather than embraced. In this particular course, taught by undergraduates, the students were asked to critically comment on fan works in public—violating the trust of the fan communities, since the students did not seek permission to do so.[1] Today, just as digital technology has enabled students of fandom to find fan work, it has also make it easier to contact and listen to fan voices from a variety of cultures. Fandom can be a diverse community, and this diversity can be manifest in what Morimoto and Chin (2013) describe as *transculturalism*, the idea that fandom crosses national and cultural borders. But the transcultural experience does not necessarily have to be global. I teach in Chicago, a city with an international population, and students come from all over the world. To create a transcultural experience, in which "affinities of affect between the fan, in his/her various contexts, and the border-crossing object" are engendered, I invite fan guest speakers into the class to speak about their experiences as fans and in Chicago fan communities (93). Local fans introduce students to contemporary fan issues like harassment at fan conventions and rape culture; they describe the way in which critical fandom influences scholarship and fandom (Mongan 2015). As a way to ethically bring fan voices into the classroom, learning from fans themselves helps illustrate specific fan mores.

By integrating fannish voices into the classroom—both my students' and the fans' themselves—my fan studies classes offer students new ways of envisioning their fannish abilities. Today, as fandom becomes more mainstream (Gray et al. 2007; Booth 2015c), our students are already working like fans. They just might not see the historical context of such activities. It's important to recognize that students are going to be producing media content—both professional and amateur—for their rest of their lives. As fan studies instructors, we can offer a historical perspective on alternate modes of creation. By offering both a historical overview of fan studies as a discipline and using fan studies as an object in and of itself in the classroom, I attempt to provide students with both the context and the contemporary fan experience.

CONCLUSION

In their collection about fan culture, Larsen and Zubernis (2012, 3) describe the tension at the heart of teaching fandom: "at the beginning of our own classes, we encourage students to embrace their inner fans. We then, of course, almost immediately tell them to stop 'squeeing' and require them to approach their chosen and perhaps newly acknowledge fandoms through a critical lens." Fan studies, as an academic subject, necessarily needs to have an air of rationality and academic rigor. But fandom is anything but: fans are emotional; they squee [Editor's note: squee is an onomatopoeia for the ecstatic glee with which fans greet the objects of their fandom] with all their vigor. They have all the feels.

This tension leads to a concern that Geraghty (2012) notes: "students, rather than seeing themselves as part of being a fan of something, take up a position of superiority. To them, fans, as the stereotypical 'passive' consumers of media texts, are cultural dupes and through a position of knowing critique students are outside observers—objective and freely detached from any emotional or personal attachment to media texts" (162). Geraghty suggests some changes for teaching university-level fan studies: "we must engage students on several levels. We must recognize the multiple fandoms that they may or may not have while also teaching them how to see themselves in the texts they are studying . . . [and we need to] break down those barriers of unfamiliarity and ignorance—start from a position of familiarity and work towards the unfamiliar" (171).

I agree with Geraghty: working with students on multiple levels engages both their academic and their fan identities. The trouble is that students are just learning their academic sides, whereas their fannish sides are already so well developed. Taking a two-tiered approach to teaching fan studies helps the two sides blend. When the scholarly and the pedagogical come together, students see fandom from the perspective of the academic and from the perspective of the fan. If, as Hills (2002) has asserted, the scholar-fan identity is problematic (inscribing value onto one or the other half of the binary), then what students do—and what the fan studies classroom should do—is present scholarship and fandom as partners, as compatriots, and as complementary forces that guide student development. Fan studies as a discipline becomes fan studies the object; and in doing so, it reaches out to erase the boundaries separating fan and student.

NOTE FOR CHAPTER 10

1. See "Comment on Delilah," Archive of Our Own (with the acknowledgment that the fluid nature of the digital environment means that comments may be deleted), http://archiveofourown.org/comments/24344573, for a discussion of the controversy.

CREATION AND ANALYSIS

Response to the Fandom and Active Audiences Class

Ashlyn Keefe

Taking a graduate level class on fandom and fan studies was not a difficult choice. In fact, it was more a question of "Why can't *every* class I take be on fandom?" At the time I enrolled, I was already a thorough Whovian (fan of *Doctor Who*) and a devotee of the then recently new BBC *Sherlock* series. I was a passionate watcher of British Channel 4's *Misfits*, and I couldn't tear myself away from *Downton Abbey*. I was, and still am, a professed fan of many texts, as well as a not-so-secret television Anglophile.

Dr. Paul Booth's two-tiered approach to the Fandom and Active Audiences class, a blend of studying the historical development of fan studies and engaging with a fan text of the student's choice, was both exciting and unnerving. As a fan who does not actively create her own fannish texts, I was leery of being pushed to not only write fan fiction but also to make a full-length fan video as a final project. Up to this point I had discussed my favorite shows and shared funny memes with friends, but I had never quite crossed the threshold and made any fannish texts of my own. It's difficult to pinpoint the reason behind my reluctance to do so, but I suspect it had more to do with my fear of failure than a lack of desire. I greatly wanted to make my own fan vid but feared that my lack of technical prowess with editing software, and the lack of quality of the software itself, would lead to a less than satisfactory product. Further dread of people not understanding or just not liking my video was also a good enough reason to never make one of my own volition. In the classroom setting, though, I had the understanding and support of my classmates and ample technical direction from Dr. Booth — he ensured that everyone had the necessary resources needed to create a fan video. I finally felt, if not 100 percent comfortable, slightly more prepared to give the whole fan video thing a try. With my fan text of choice in hand, BBC's *Sherlock*, I was ready to become one very active fan.

The framework for the Fandom and Active Audiences class did much to set our study of fandom apart from the other graduate-level media and cinema studies courses. Engaging with and taking ownership of our fannish texts while situated in the historical context of fan studies gave us a new angle of approach from the typical scholarly academic role: as much objectivity as possible and a critical stance for studying film and television. But this viewpoint was different. This wasn't looking critically at, for instance, a film that I'd never seen or a television show that I kind of liked. This was taking a critical eye and playing with a media text that was near and dear to my heart. This firm push toward engaging in fannish activity, far beyond the little that I did before, was one of the most effective parts of the class. It in fact proved to be some of the most enjoyable and memorable experiences I had while pursuing my graduate degree.

You can discuss fan activities. You can talk about the different kinds of fan fiction there are, and maybe look at some examples. You can watch excellent fan videos for any fannish or cult text in existence on YouTube. We did in fact watch some in class. But it is one thing to analyze these examples of fan activities and another to fully engage with them—including writing your own slash (which I did) and splicing together your very own fan vid (which I learned is a terribly involved and time-consuming investment). But the key element Dr. Booth had us undertake was a thorough analysis of our own fannish creations. This twofold process of in-depth creation and objective yet subjective analysis of our own fan creations masterfully coerced us into a critical engagement with our fan texts.

Most fans are quick to react when their media text is criticized, whether or not the criticisms are true or false. In light of this, the materials on the aca-fan and the myriad class discussions we had on inhabiting that uneasy space were key points of the class for me. As a graduate student, I was automatically part of the insular academic world, privy to certain theories of popular culture, critical media theories, and ethnographical literature. There is no way to remove oneself from the critical study of a text when the text in question happens to be one that you love. It is difficult, perhaps impossible, for any scholar to completely separate him- or herself from the text being studied. We are all human, after all, and no matter how hard you may strive for objectivity, an analysis can never be totally free from some level of subjectivity. This, of course, is all the more heightened when studying your beloved fan text.

As a fan, I am emotionally bound to my text. So counter to my academic self, I have also my fan self, which is party to the particular knowledge and traditions of the community. According to Dr. Booth, these two different positions are often at odds with each other—fans tend to work outside the traditional education system, and academics within. Or there is the struggle of the division between high and low culture, in which academics and their opinions must always be taken as the final answer because of their scholarly standing. Meanwhile, the devoted fan is played off as unable to truly analyze the text. However, Dr. Booth's passionate lectures and involved class discussions did a great deal to merge these two perspectives, with the result that my classmates and I concluded that our fandom and our scholarship are in fact one and the same. It is a matter of learning to merge both our academic and our fan methods of critique and analysis and, most important, of remembering that there is no one true expert on the subject.

There were so many other thoroughly engaging and thought-provoking aspects of the class that I could easily write more about them. But the lasting impression I took away from the class is that fan studies is as important and necessary a field of discipline as ever in today's media environment. It's not that I doubted the validity of studying fandom—I simply didn't comprehend how critical this kind of work is in today's media environment. As fan culture becomes ever more a part of mainstream culture, it's essential that we analyze the often uncriticized practices of the norm. Thanks to the Fandom and Active Audiences class, I've been inspired to keep on doing so, and I might even make a couple more fan vids while I'm at it.

APPENDIX A

INTERVIEW WITH PRIYADHARSHINI SEETHARAMAN

In this interview on her experience in Katherine Anderson Howell's remix classroom, ReWriting *Jane Eyre*, Priya Seetharaman, a sophomore, speaks about the fandom classroom. The interview was conducted at George Washington University on July 17, 2015. Priya's reflections gave shape to the presentation "Remix in the Classroom: A Student Perspective" at the National Conference of the Popular Culture Association in March 2016, and ultimately led to the inspiration for the introduction of this volume.

Katherine: Did you have to grit your teeth to get through [the course]? Or did it get better [than what you expected of university writing]?

Priya: It definitely got better, I think because I realized that even though we had to read *Jane Eyre*, the stuff we were writing about and researching wasn't always necessarily directly pertinent to *Jane Eyre*. I thought I'd have to do a whole lot more character analysis and talk about the relationship between Jane and her mother, her lack of parents or [her relationship] with her father and her instable childhood, or something like that. I was not interested in Jane; I did not care about her. I just wasn't interested in her life. If she was a real person, I'd probably be like "Okay, bye." Unfortunately, because I am a mean person, I would just leave her crying and walk away.

But then, as we went through the whole writing process and learned how to choose a topic and figure out what we were interested in, I realized I could explore the relationship: generalize Jane as a middle-class, maybe lower-middle-class woman who didn't have any sort of family or anything, and her relationship with [Edward] Rochester, a man from an aristocratic background, with that kind of power and age difference, and how that sort of dynamic played out. I've always realized I like this. Those kinds of relationships have fascinated me. And then I realized I could talk about that instead of talking about how sad Jane was or how pathetic I thought she was.

Katherine: Did anything carry over into the spring semester to your biomedical engineering [courses]?

Priya: Things carried over very broadly and generally. Right now I'm working in a research lab. I'm gonna give background about what we do in the lab. We're looking at infrared images of the breasts of patients with breast cancer, because when breast cancer happens, there's a region of growth. And you can see that growth in this infrared image because that area is warmer than the area around it. That's the goal [we have]; that's what we want to achieve.

But the question is how to write the program to do it. There're all these different methods, and one thing that really carried over from UW [university writing] was that you don't have to always look at people who write about *Jane Eyre*. You don't always have to look at people who write about the romantic relationships between a young woman and an older man. You can look at other sorts of economic relationships; you can look at these other elements in the Jane and Rochester relationship—other elements of *Jane Eyre*, and that's what carried over to my research.

I realized I didn't really have to look at people who studied breast cancer. I didn't really have to look at people who did image analysis of thermographic images. I could look at random fractal designs, people who generated images, who did other sorts of image analysis in other applications, and use that math, use those methods, and apply them to mine because that's where the research happens. That's how you make your research paper, whether in English or in engineering, different.

Katherine: This is a very proud moment for me to hear you say that. I'm very, very proud.

Priya: The course in general just taught me how to think, which is probably the most important thing that it could teach you. And it taught me how to think—this is going to sound so cliché—but think outside the box, how to approach a problem from different angles. It doesn't have to have a direct link, but something that you find in some other researchers' work can help you find a method to explore what you're exploring.

Katherine: So eventually, you came to the remix as part of the course. We talked about concepts of fan fiction, concepts of fan writing and fan practices. And you were very honest with me and told me that you were not a fan of *Jane Eyre*, so I wanted to know what was it like to remix or rewrite something that you really were not all that into.

Priya: It was really weird, because I had to write from Jane's point of view. That was the hardest thing, probably, I've ever done, because I had to make myself be Jane, pretend I was Jane, and feel all of Jane's inner emotions as an older person looking back on her younger years and reflecting on herself. So first I had to become young Jane, and then I had to make myself grow up and become older Jane. And then I had to make older Jane look at younger Jane and think about how she would reflect on her life, and that was really difficult for me.

At some point, I just had to sit down and write it and rewrite it until I was in a certain mood, where I felt like I was an old Jane and was able to write that. I don't use drugs, but I feel like I was probably in some sort of high or like some sort of state that allowed me to do that, and I don't think I can ever return to that state again. It's a onetime thing. I honestly wrote most of that piece in one sitting. I revised it, but I could never go back; I don't think I could ever go back and rewrite it.

Katherine: That's really interesting, because you spent a lot of time in my office wrestling with those ideas. I can't remember exactly where you started, but you went through a lot before you got there. And it sounds like you had to find a zen moment. Obviously, it was strange to get into that zen place, but was it more stressful than other kinds of work that you had done? Or was it just a different experience?

Priya: Both. It is definitely different, because for any of my other classes, or any of the other stuff that I do with my life, it is science based or math based. I've just always kinda had an affinity toward that. I've just always liked math; like math is my thing. One time I think I invented some math in my sleep! It is always easy for me to do math. It is always easy for me to think about those [math problems] because I'm always ready to think about those and figure out how to solve this problem or find some procedure to do this or something—to conduct an experiment or something.

But with writing, I don't really have that affinity. I don't, and with English, I'm not always in a place where I can notice the details and understand some metaphor or understand the higher meaning behind just the text that I see. So a lot of times, especially the first time I read *Jane Eyre*, the first time reading it through, I would just read it and take everything at face value, because that's often the state I was in when I was reading it at like two in the morning or something.

So that's how I would initially take in everything. It took me awhile to realize that what you think you understand is not actually what's happening. You probably need to sit down and actually maybe draw some things out or like talk about it with some people and figure out what they're actually trying to say.

And so because I had to do that—not just when I was reading and trying to understand material, but also when I was writing—often I'd start writing, and I'd keep writing. And I'd go back and I'd read it. I [was] like, "Okay this doesn't make sense."

It took me, I think, most of the course—yeah, definitely most of the course, because nothing clicked for me until that last Wednesday or Thursday when I sat down and I was like, "Okay, I'm gonna give myself twenty-four hours to just read this whole thing." And I understood what I was missing, which pieces of evidence that I needed to back up my argument, or what kind of arguments I was looking for. But if those arguments didn't exist, then they didn't exist and I had to change my ideas.

It was stressful. And sometimes the deadline would work. Sometimes the pressure of having the deadline would force me to get into this sort of state where I could see evidence in ... boxes and I would be able to connect them to my ideas and make a bigger box. And in my head, evidence works as like a stem and leaf plot [a way of organizing data in mathematics], if that's the term, or like a tree, maybe, where I'm looking for the little leaves and then I work my way to the branches and then the trunk, which is the main idea or my final opinion or argument that I have to make. Except it really doesn't look like a tree. It looks like boxes.

It was difficult to get into that space because like I mentioned, I just was not used to seeing evidence like that or looking for research, looking for evidence in other papers like that. And I think that has a lot to do with me at first just kind of thumping out my ideas and being like "Here's what I think."

And first I think how my brain, how my process works, is just dumping out what I think about everything. And then [I] kind of figur[e] out which parts of my arguments need some sort of evidence, either from the actual original *Jane Eyre* text itself or from some other outside source describing social, political, and economic relationships.

Katherine: So you ended up writing this rewrite that was a little bit closer to [an] alternate universe, sort of bordering on real-person fiction. I think you wrote [about] Jane responding to the negative review of the book instead of Charlotte [Brontë]. Why? How did you end up there? I mean, I remember you going through all of this, but why did that seem important to you, as opposed to what some of your classmates may have done[, such as] tell the story from Rochester's perspective?

Priya: Well, I think for me, when I got to the end of the book and I finished reading it and put the book down, I didn't see any sort of personal development from Jane. I didn't have any sort of validation from her that she had progressed at all, and so I needed that. I needed to see something where she came full circle, or some sort of justification that she was happy. Because I think the book ended ... it wasn't like the entire book was written in [the] third person, but it seemed very omniscient. I didn't feel any sort of personal connection with Jane. And it seemed like we were just leaving her, rather than seeing her through to a good comfortable place in her life. Not that all books have to end happy, but this one seemed to end happy, so I wanted to make sure she was okay.

But also Jane is ... as we talked about, she came from kind of nowhere; she came from nothing, she had no family, and she ends up marrying Rochester and having a family of her own. But I still felt like, because she was alone for most of her childhood, that she was very self-reliant. She [had to] have been self-reliant to be that strong to go through and live through all those experiences that she had at Lowood. And so I thought that the most natural thing for Jane to do was to look to herself and have a conversation with herself and ask, "Am I actually doing okay? Am I actually happy? Is this something? Are these choices I'm making good for me and will I ... will I not just be happy now but also be happy later, like five or ten years down the road?"

I thought Jane wouldn't really be mature enough to ask those questions of herself. That's why I wanted to look at Jane five, ten, or fifteen years down the road, because at that point she'd have the maturity and experience to go back and look at her life and reflect upon it. [I had] Jane write from her current state of mind at forty years old—I think that's how old I had her—and reflect on her life; and I think initially that's what my first, second, or possibly even third draft had her doing.

Katherine: Yeah, you wrote a lot of drafts. You were in my office two days a week with something new! I was happy to see you.

Priya: I don't know if I was happy to be here all the time.

Katherine: You were very frustrated.

Priya: I was frustrated. I was frustrated that I couldn't get the answer. I wanted to find the answer.

First, I had Jane reflecting on her life and just kind of giving a sort of prologue to her autobiography, her autobiography being the entire *Jane Eyre* novel itself. I just wanted to write a little prelude to that. I thought that'd be a cute little interesting and exciting idea to give some sort of insight to Jane as an older woman. That ended up being very dry and boring, because there's no conflict in her life happening at that stage; or at least I'd like to think that there [was] no conflict happening at that point. She wouldn't have [had] any motivation to just be like "Okay . . . well I'm happy now! Thanks for reading. Come have some tea with me sometime!" She's not gonna write that, and I realized, after I wrote the draft and went and looked at it, "This is so boring. We need to have some kind of conflict here."

So I went back and looked at Jane. And she went through many bad situations. There were certainly points in her life when she was beaten down and prevented from expressing her opinions. But there were other times where she was definitely vocal and outwardly expressive about people who were rude to her, who were mean, who mistreated others. And I felt that when she [was] forty and in a happy state and living a happy life, she would regain that confidence because she knows that being outwardly expressive about her views would not hurt her because she's firmly established, not just in her romantic life but also her family life. And even economically because she's now a writer; socially because she's married into Rochester's family.

And so because she has that sort of stability in her life, I concluded that she would be able to express herself again, that she would be able to have strong opinions and argue with other people because she knew that she wouldn't be hurt like she was before.

And so that's where I had this idea of Jane needing to argue with someone. Then the question became "Who should she argue with?" This is where I went through the back of the book and looked at things from Charlotte Brontë's life; there [are] many theories that Brontë modeled Jane after her own life. So starting from that theory, I went to look and see what Brontë did, and I found this letter in the back of the book that was a response from Brontë to her critics. I was like "What! This sounds like a good idea. Let's see where it takes me." And that's how I ended up writing as a forty-year-old Jane responding to critics of her life.

Also because people were always critiquing Jane about her life and about her behavior, she gets some satisfaction from responding to this critic because she's finally able to respond on an equal level. And she's in a place where her response to the critic will be taken just as seriously as the critics' opinions themselves because she's no longer a child arguing against an adult or some orphan from a low-class family arguing against her nurse; she's an established author and successful and, at least socially, established woman who is arguing. I think that is also like [a] "fuck you" to the world [that] gave her this terrible circumstance to grow up in that she ended up doing okay.

Katherine: You once said in a group workshop something about not feeling like you were allowed to adapt. Do you still feel that way? Do you feel like you have more authority with source material now?

Priya: Ah, yeah! I started to realize it after I started comparing it to science because that's how stuff makes sense to me. In science, you can take someone else's methods, or you can take someone else's end goal, and you can approach it from a different way. So you don't have to cure cancer, or you don't have to cure cancer with this one particular drug; you can try another drug; you can try using ultrasound; you can try using all kinds of things and there's many ways to achieve that one end goal. Likewise, you don't have to use ultrasound just to see babies; you can use it as a cure; you can use it as another tool. And so when I started to realize that, I saw that you don't have to take source material, original works as is; you can take their goal and see what is another way that they could have achieved this goal.

Like Harry Potter. How else could Harry have killed Voldemort? Is Harry even necessary to kill Voldemort? You could probably have had someone else kill Voldemort; probably Neville could have done a perfectly good job of killing Voldemort. That would have been a wonderful ending.

So when I started seeing that, I was like "Oh, this is, this is kind of okay, like it is fine to like play around with these ideas." I think a lot of fan writing especially—because of, you know, like Fanfiction.net and everything ... it's not for other people really; it's kind of more for yourself.

When I was trying to think of some sort of topic to write [about for] my final paper on *Jane Eyre*, I knew that if I tried to figure out something for a paper and write it down, it wasn't going to fly well; it was not going to happen, and it wasn't going to be pretty, and I wasn't going to do well, and it just wasn't going to be satisfying. So I had to find something that I needed from the book. That's kind of how it works with science: you don't just try to find a cure for something, or you don't try to find some method because you just need to find a method. You find it, you go and look for it, because you have an interest in finding a better way to optimize something or you have an interest in finding a way to compress images better and transport them better.

So going back to Fanfiction.net—reading those stories published online.... Yeah, they're published because people want to share them with other people, see how other people react to them, and bond with others and talk about characters and how things potentially could have gone or should have gone. But a lot of that writing and that process is more for the authors themselves, and it definitely helps. It definitely helps the writer understand the characters or understand the novel or the story itself more.

Like now, even though I still don't like *Jane Eyre* and I still don't like Jane, after writing the paper, I realize "Okay, this is why you did everything. I probably would have done the same in your situation. I probably would have done worse in your situation. I still don't like you; you're still a little bitch sometimes, but it's fine. I understand and I kind of sympathize with you a little bit."

So because it helps authors and writers—well, not authors, I should say writers—reach that understanding, I think adaptation is okay.

Katherine: So *Jane Eyre* is a very white, very British colonial text, right? There is literally Indian colonialism written into the text. How [did] you respond to that [as a student of Indian heritage]? What [did] you feel about that? Was that uncomfortable for you in the class? Did you care?

Priya: I didn't care. I think it was mostly because I knew the context of the book and the time Brontë was writing in. Because at that time England was colonizing everything! "Let's colonize Africa! Let's colonize India! Let's colonize the world!" So because I've seen a whole lot of documentaries about England colonizing India and other places, I just understood the imperialist mindset. Maybe if there were characters of other races, if there were characters [of color] in the novel, prominent characters [of color] in the novel, I would have reacted differently and had like some sort of emotional response, and that's what I probably would have ended up writing about. But there weren't any major moments where race was a feature.

I knew everyone [of the major characters] was supposed to be white and that they were all going to be white because Brontë was also a middle-class white woman. And that's what she would have noticed and wanted to write about, and her audience was also, again, maybe aristocratic, maybe middle-class people, who had time to read and who could read, which were, again, white people.

APPENDIX B

SYLLABI AND COURSE DESIGN

Syllabi frame the key principles of the remix or fandom classroom for students. The following syllabi, from Roberson and Grady (chapter 3) and Booth (chapter 10), provide examples of how to design and structure a course to make the purpose of remix methods clear and delineate the ethics of the fandom classroom.

Roberson and Grady begin by explaining the significance of the media text, *The Shawshank Redemption,* and the associated fan pilgrimage site, the Shawshank Trail. They detail the purpose of studying fans in a service learning course, including guiding questions for students to consider. In their weekly schedule, included here, they provide a sense of how a complex, interdisciplinary, fan-centered course can function. Finally, I have also chosen to include the elements of their surveys of fans here as a model of how to communicate with fans when researching.

Booth's syllabus provides an example of how to familiarize students with fans and fandom as cultural concepts and provides a course rationale to explain what a course studying these concepts offers to students. The rationale makes it clear what precisely students will do in the course and how those activities parallel fannish practices. Like all syllabi, Booth's offers goals, objectives, and readings. Here, these sections avoid institutional language and instead straightforwardly communicate the things students will learn about fandom. In the included breakdown of assignments, readers can see the ways that these assignments offer a clear developmental structure and a forward trajectory, something to consider in course design.

GRADY AND ROBERSON SYLLABUS
DR. MAURA GRADY
HN 390: INTERDISCIPLINARY SEMINAR (THEME: OHIO);
FALL 2013
The Shawshank Redemption Unit, Fan Culture, and Film Tourism in Ohio

Director and screenwriter Frank Darabont's 1994 film *The Shawshank Redemption* was adapted from the Stephen King novella "Rita Hayworth and Shawshank Redemption," originally published in the collection *Different Seasons* in 1982. The screenplay attracted a talented cast and crew to the project, which settled on Mansfield, Ohio, for the "home base" of its film production, given the suitability of the Ohio State Reformatory as the location for the prison in the film. Other sequences were shot in Ashland, Mansfield, Upper Sandusky, and Malabar Farms, and hundreds of local residents were involved in the 1993 filming. Although the novella and the film are set in Maine, as are many of King's works, the real history and atmosphere of these Ohio locations, as well as the contributions of the north-central Ohio communities, have a real effect on the look and feel of the film, and the production has had a lasting impact on our local area [Ashland, Mansfield, and Wyandot Counties in Ohio].

Although the film did not do well at the box office upon its release in 1994, it was nominated for seven Academy Awards and has since gained a large following through showings on cable and through home video rentals. It has consistently been voted the number one movie of all time by the users of the Internet Movie Database (Imdb.com). Like other initially ignored classics, it has become a beloved favorite of millions of viewers.

The Shawshank Trail—organized by the Shawshank Woodshop in Upper Sandusky, the Mansfield Convention and Visitors Bureau, and others—was developed in response to requests by fans for information on the filming sites of *The Shawshank Redemption*. Jodie Puster, the group tour and media director for the Mansfield-Richland CVB, notes that the tour grew out of the CVB's desire to help fans find what they wanted to see. Eventually, fourteen sites were added to the trail; a brochure, a website, and a Facebook page were developed; and unique products were made available for purchase at selected sites. The sites are marked with a distinctive logo, and podcasts are available online for a self-guided audio tour. This year [2013, the year of the course], the CVB has organized a three-day twentieth-anniversary celebration event over Labor Day weekend, complete with special events and celebrity guests.

I am collaborating with Dr. Richard "Robby" Roberson, a colleague in Hospitality Management and Tourism (in the College of Business) to study the success of the Shawshank Trail in providing fans with a satisfying experience. Working with fans and learning from fan responses, we will all study how the organizers of the trail have expanded and enhanced it as a tourism destination for fans, and we will survey fans to measure their ranking of various quantitative factors such as expectations, satisfaction, and qualitative factors such as the personal meaning the sites and event hold for them as fans of the film.

That's where you come in! We are hoping that as many of you as possible will be able to attend the events over Labor Day weekend and to speak with fans who are visiting the Shawshank Trail. The work you do on this, and your written reflections (on the readings, the film, the novella, and your experience) will constitute the bulk of your points for this unit.

This is an opportunity for you to study a piece of local Ohio history (the filming sites have their own stories to tell), as well as local businesses, local and regional tourism practices, fan culture theory and practice, local film history, local theater, and local film production. Your reflection (to be completed at the end of the unit) will require you to focus on some aspect of the unit that has personal or professional resonance for you and to research the context for your reflection. There will be no cost to students for participating in this project, and transportation can be provided.

Week One

In our first week, you will view the film, complete some background reading, study the Shawshank Trail materials, and attend a special tour (just for our group) of the Ohio State Reformatory in Mansfield. Our guide will be the reformatory's head archivist, Shannon Lusk. She studied popular culture at Bowling Green State University and focuses on history and material culture, or the use of artifacts to help tell the stories of people and places. This tour will focus less on the film and more on the real and fascinating history of this location. We will also plan the logistics of the reunion weekend and the conducting of surveys.

There is currently no scheduled group screening for the film, but I'm happy to arrange that if we can find a time that a number of students can attend—Tuesday, Wednesday, or Thursday night of week one, perhaps? If you are not able to attend a screening, you can view the film in the library on your own schedule, find it legally online, or rent the DVD.

Week Two

In our second week we will gear up for the reunion, discuss and research the fan base for the film, and discuss your responses to the film. The fan surveys will be conducted during this weekend at several locations. Class on Friday will be spent conducting surveys in Ashland, Mansfield, Upper Sandusky, and Malabar Farms.

Week Three

In this short week (Monday, September 2, is a university holiday) we will process the collected quantitative data and discuss the qualitative responses gathered at the reunion, and you will begin writing reflections on your experiences interacting with the filming locations, the fans, and the members of the cast and crew. We will also discuss the novella toward the end of the week.

Week Four

Students will complete the individual research required for their reflections and present them to the class.

Some (Not All!) of Our Guiding Questions

What is a fan? Do fans *have* to participate in communal activities? Who are the fans of *Shawshank*? How do fans behave? Why do fans want to visit filming locations? What are fans looking for? What is unique about the fans of *Shawshank* and/or Stephen King?

Shawshank Trail Survey 2013 Questions
A. Section 1. Demographics
    1. Age _____
    2. Sex____
    3. How many are in your party?_____
        Whom did you come with?_____
    4. Where are you from? What is the zip code? _____
    5. Have you ever visited any other events related to films? Yes   No
        How many?_____
    6. How did you become aware of this event? (Check all that apply.)
        Family_____
        Friends _____
        TV, radio, or newspaper _____

    Google search _____
    Social media _____
    Other Internet _____
    Other _____
  7. Do you think you'd come back to the trail again?
  8. Would you be more interested/ less interested/ no change to visit filming sites of other films?
B. Section 2. Open-Ended Questions
  1. What made you decide to make the trip?
  2. Can you tell me your Shawshank story? (What makes this movie special to you?)
  3. What was the most important part of coming here for you?
  4. Have you had the chance to talk to other people in your everyday life about this movie a lot? Is that something you've done here this weekend?
C. Section 3. Importance-Satisfaction Scale
  1. On a scale of 1 to 10, rate the following factors regarding the Shawshank trail with 1 being the least and 10 being the most. How important is each of the following?
      _____ (1-10) Interacting with participants (actors, extras, crew) in making the movie
      _____ (1-10) Visiting the filming locations
      _____ (1-10) Interacting with other fans of the movie
      _____ (1-10) Obtaining merchandise and memorabilia related to the movie
      _____ (1-10) Interacting with locations or props, such as by taking pictures, touching, or manipulating
  2. On a scale of 1 to 10, rate the following factors regarding the Shawshank trail with 1 being the least and 10 being the most. How satisfied were you with the following?
      _____ (1-10) Interacting with participants (actors, extras, crew) in making the movie
      _____ (1-10) Visiting the filming locations
      _____ (1-10) Interacting with other fans of the movie
      _____ (1-10) Obtaining merchandise and memorabilia related to the movie
      _____ (1-10) Interacting with locations or props, such as by taking pictures, touching, or manipulating

3. On a scale of 1 to 10, rate the following, regarding the Shawshank trail with 1 being the least and 10 being the most. How important is this movie to you? (1-10)_____

Shawshank Trail Survey 2014 Questions
What is your home ZIP code?
Did you buy themed merchandise today?
If yes, what?
What were you most looking forward to in coming to this event?
Why and how is this movie important to you?
Have you ever visited another filming site?
If yes, how does this compare?
If this event is held again, is Labor Day a good weekend to do it?

IRB Script for Shawshank Trail Surveys Consent Form

Hello—I am a researcher, professor, student [choose one] at Ashland University. We are conducting research on fan experiences with the Shawshank Trail. If you agree, I would like to ask you some questions about your experiences and perceptions regarding the Shawshank anniversary weekend. The survey should take three to four minutes. Your responses are confidential.

Your responses may be recorded. Your participation is voluntary. You can decline to participate, and you can stop your participation at any time, if you wish to do so, without any negative consequences to you.

If you have any questions or concerns about the research, please feel free to contact Dr. Robby Roberson at (419) 289-5930, or at office 230 at 401 College Avenue, Ashland, Ohio.

Do you have any questions about the research project?

COURSE SYLLABUS AND READINGS FOR FANDOM AND ACTIVE AUDIENCES
DR. PAUL BOOTH

Course Description

This course introduces students to the world of media fandom. Fans hold an emotional attachment to media texts and often act on it. By investigating the types of media texts people connect to, as well as the work fans do in their community, students encounter new ways of participating with media.

Students not only examine fans historically but also examine media from the point of view of a fan. This course looks at how participating in fandom can aid the development of diversity and positive social change.

Course Rationale

Fans hold an emotional attachment to a particular object: in this class, we will be looking specifically at *fans of visual and textual popular culture*. Audiences make meaning from the media texts that are presented to them: from *Star Trek* to *Buffy the Vampire Slayer*, from *Leave It to Beaver* to *Friends*, audiences read media texts in a variety of surprising, and often fascinating, ways. Fans take this implicit rewriting of media texts one step further, since they often rewrite their version of the media text in their own way.

Although fans have been writing fan fiction since at least the time of Sir Arthur Conan Doyle's Sherlock Holmes stories, recent technological advances have led to a variety of new forms of this art. Whether writing fiction, creating videos, role-playing on social network sites, or using other unique types of digital writing, fans are exploring the Web in amazing ways. Furthermore, we as a media-saturated society have seen more media products developed to cater to this fan crowd. From long-form cult television shows like *Gossip Girls*, *Sleepy Hollow*, or *Supernatural* to viral marketing campaigns to spread interest in a film, our media texts are becoming facets of this age of the fan.

This class takes seriously the work of fans in our media society and studies the work they do as critical and meaningful media products in their own right. We do not assume that fan fiction is less worthy than mainstream media products; rather, it contributes to an ongoing discussion of the uses of media technology. We also explore fandom as a metaphor for the cultural work going on all over the Web. Students both research and produce fan-based works and will be expected to create analyses of fandom and creative works of fan fiction of their own.

Course Goals

This course has three main goals. The first is to gain a better *understanding* of fandom as a historical concept in cultural theory. The second is to gain the ability to *analyze* the production, distribution, and consumption of media texts in today's media-rich environment. The third is to *critique* the methods and types of fan-created fiction in new media.

Course Objectives

At the end of this course, students will be able to do the following:

> Create fannish texts
> Critique their own and other peoples' writing
> Demonstrate an understanding of the theory behind studying fans and fandom
> Synthesize lessons and readings in a video project

Class Readings

To buy (DePaul bookstore or online): Jenkins, Henry. *Textual Poachers: Television Fans and Participatory Culture*. 2nd ed. New York: Routledge, 2012.

Recommended reading: Booth, Paul. *Playing Fans: Negotiating Fandom and Media in the Digital Age*. Iowa City: University of Iowa Press, 2015.

Stein, Louisa. *Millennial Fandom*. Iowa City: University of Iowa Press, 2015.

Any of Intellect Books's Fan Phenomena series (chapters to be assigned upon purchase).

Topics: Audrey Hepburn, *Batman*, *Big Lebowski*, *Buffy the Vampire Slayer*, *Doctor Who*, *The Hunger Games*, Jane Austen, Marilyn Monroe, *The Rocky Horror Picture Show*, Sherlock Holmes, *Star Trek*, *Star Wars*, *Supernatural*, and *Twin Peaks*.

Grading

Your grade is based on 600 points:

> Media analysis: 100 points
> Fan analysis: 100 points
> Fan fiction: 100 points
> Fan video and presentation: 100 points
> Final Tumblr analysis: 100 points
> Participation: 100 points

Assignments

In this class you will have the opportunity to spend the full quarter investigating one particular aspect of media fandom that interests you. You will pick a media text that you want to follow for the quarter. This can be a television show, a film (or film series), a book (or book series), a video game, or another media text. Each paper or project builds on the ones that came before, so make sure to pick something interesting that you won't get bored working on for all ten weeks.

In addition, as part of this class, you will maintain a Tumblr account that follows the media text you are investigating. You should start the Tumblr account when you have chosen your media text and work on it throughout the quarter. Students that currently have Tumblr accounts should start a new account rather than use their current one. You should begin by following about five people or blogs, and by the end of the quarter you should augment this with many more (at least seven more). You do not have to post your fan fiction or fan video on Tumblr, but you may if you'd like to. Therefore, you should maintain this Tumblr account throughout the course and check it at least every day to make sure you are keeping current. You should feel free to follow more people as you continue in class; the best Tumblr accounts have a variety of sources. Your Tumblr account will be a record of some contemporary fan practices that you can contrast with the historical view of fandom we'll take in this class.

Your main project will start with an analysis of a cult text in a traditional or mass medium (book, television series, film, video game) that you find interesting. Examine this text for the narrative, plot, characters, locations, and other areas that fans might be able to take hold of and attach themselves to. Note: This is not a plot summary, but an analysis of the ways in which fans might use this media text. For example, you might look at the *Star Trek* series and note how the long narrative, multiple media texts, many characters, and otherworldliness of the series allow fans to take root among the scenes. You will use your Tumblr account to augment this analysis, which should be around fifteen hundred words.

After this you will be asked to write your own fan fiction story about the media text that you've analyzed. You should write an interesting, creative entry in the fan fiction canon. You may write whatever type of fan fiction story you like, but you must connect it to the extant text in some manner. Your story should be text based (written like a short story). Also, give your paper to a beta reader to read (this can be someone you know). For example, you might write your own slash *Star Trek* fiction about Lieutenant Commander Data and Captain Picard finding love in an interesting manner. This story should be around two thousand words. You will also write a one-thousand-word analysis of your story that describes how it connects to the media text and offers historical context for the genre of fan fiction.

Your next assignment will be a critical reading and analysis of some fan-created work. You should read a work of fan fiction already written or produced about your media text, find a fan video of your media text, and compare these to your Tumblr account. You should compare and contrast the way the authors of these texts read the main text: How do they interpret it? What are the important components for each author? Finally, point out additional moments in your cult text that the authors could have used for their creative works. For example, you might look at fan fiction written about *Star Trek* and find that this is a Mary Sue story that examines the character of Uhura in a new light, and compare it to a slash video of Kirk/Spock. This analysis should be around fifteen hundred words.

You will be asked to create a fan video, and this project will integrate everything you've learned so far. Your video should be three to five minutes long. You can make a vid (i.e., reedit scenes from your text set to music), a fan-created adaption, or any other type of video. In addition, you will be asked to turn in a 750-word statement that outlines how this work fits within the topics of the class and the media text you've chosen, and you will be asked to present this final project to the class. In this presentation you will describe how it fits within the canon of the extant media text and the steps you took to create it. The video project is worth one hundred points. For example, you could make a mash-up video of *Star Trek* characters that illustrates Data and Picard falling in love, or you could make a fiction video starring you and your friends.

Your final analysis, which should be integrated into your final video presentation, is to analyze your Tumblr experience as a *community of voices*. You should read Tumblr as a conversation with different viewpoints about the media text. Your final analysis of one thousand words should look at the different viewpoints, ideas, objects, and arguments the people who are contributing to Tumblr are creating. Analyze the communities of Tumblr, using the Stein and Booth readings as your guide.

APPENDIX C

ASSIGNMENTS

The fandom classroom requires thoughtful assignment design. Assignments using fannish methods in an academic setting walk a fine line between play, creative freedom, and passionate textual engagement on the one hand, and rigor, essential scholarly texts, and skill and knowledge building on the other. In this appendix I offer Smol's assignment (chapter 1) as a guide for striking this balance in the face-to-face classroom, and Aronsson, Fjordevik, and Inose's (chapter 6) for a guide in online courses. Both offer clear guidelines that allow for freedom and self-direction. Both demonstrate the opportunity for students to build skill and knowledge in subject areas and to play with the canonical material.

WINTER TERM PROJECTS ASSIGNMENTS (SMOL)

We will extend our concepts of medievalism in the second term to include other modes of adaptation and a look at the cultural study of fandom. The suggestions below represent possible lines of inquiry for your second-term projects, but it is up to you to define your individual project. I would expect you to work with any of the readings on the syllabus this term. You should discuss your ideas with me before the February study break at least once. All topics will require a presentation to the class. These are the suggestions:

1. Do a creative adaptation of Tolkien's work. Paint a picture, write a story, make a video, direct a play, or perform some music. The project should be accompanied by a well-researched analysis (two thousand words minimum) that situates your adaptation in relation to relevant critical discussions of adaptation, fandom, Tolkien's fiction, or other relevant topics.

2. Do a literary analysis of Tolkien's own adaptations in his fiction. Discuss your selected text in a well-researched essay (three thousand words minimum) that presents your reading of the text in the context of current critical opinions on Tolkien and adaptation.
3. Do an analysis of literature film adaptation by discussing Tolkien's text and any of the film adaptations. You will need to develop your own focused and interesting topic that includes an analysis of relevant film elements. This should be a well-researched piece of work (three thousand words minimum) that presents your own analysis of the text and the films in the context of current critical opinions on Tolkien and film adaptation.
4. Do a critical analysis of fan adaptations of Tolkien's works. Select a mode of creativity usually defined as belonging to fandom, such as artwork, fiction, music videos, costume play, or gaming. This should be a well-researched piece of work (three thousand words minimum) that presents your own analysis of the activity in the context of current critical opinions on fandom, adaptation, and Tolkien.

All of the above projects will have to be submitted in the following stages:

Design: 40 Percent of the Project Grade

Think of this portion of your assignment as a research process log that records the steps you have gone through in researching and planning your project. It will be easiest if you record all stages of your project step-by-step, including the date of your activity and a clear account in full sentences of what you did; for example, did you talk to other people about a possible topic? What secondary sources did you look for? Where did you find them: in a library catalogue, in a database, on the library shelves, or on the Web? Did you need to ask for help in finding sources? What ideas did you play around with based on your readings? Along the way, did you try some freewriting, brainstorming, or outlining? If relevant to your project, did you make preliminary sketches or create a storyboard? Record your dead ends as well as your discoveries—they are all part of the research design process. Everyone should submit an individual design log even if he or she is working collaboratively with others.

The part one submission is due March 5. Your design log at this stage should be a fairly detailed document of at least fifteen hundred words charting your research and creative progress. You should have a definite idea of what your topic or creative product will be. You should have some ideas about what you need to do to get to the final submission (i.e., what books you still want to read, what research topics you still need to understand, and what creative processes you still need to go through). You should include an annotated bibliography of the secondary sources you have read to this point. Annotations should be in correct MLA style.

The part two submission is due March 26. Your design log at this point should continue an account of your research and creative progress in a fairly detailed narrative of at least 1000 words. Your design log at this point should also include the relevant element for your project from the following:

1. For research essays: a thesis and a detailed abstract for your planned essay
2. For art projects: a working sketch with an account of techniques to be used
3. For video projects: a storyboard of planned shots and a working script
4. For creative writing projects: a summary of the story, a list of characters, and a clear account of the style you are planning to write in, with at least one draft paragraph of the final work
5. For music projects: a clear account of the musical style and techniques to be used, as well as any lyrics that you are planning to include in your performance or recording.

Please consult with me about requirements if you are planning a different kind of project from the ones outlined above.

Criteria for evaluation: correct grammar, spelling, punctuation, and documentation of sources; a clear and detailed account of how you found secondary sources and how you are planning to use them (or why you are not planning to use certain ones); and a design plan that culminates in the appropriate elements, as outlined above.

Craft: 25 Percent of the Project Grade

Craft refers to how well you execute your design plan in your final project. Do you interest and engage your reader, spectator, or listener?

The criteria for evaluation are effective techniques used to engage the reader, listener, or spectator; correct grammar, spelling, and punctuation in the written analysis; and correct documentation of sources in the written analysis.

Insight: 25 Percent of the Project Grade

This portion of the final project refers to how interesting and intellectually stimulating your ideas are. Do you make good use of secondary sources? Do you develop a clearly defined thesis or focus that presents your ideas in an intellectually stimulating light?

The criteria for evaluation are a well-defined thesis or focus for the project or written analysis that leads to an interesting presentation of the topic; and effective use of the best secondary sources available to stimulate ideas and support the presentation of the topic.

The written analysis for all projects and any creative productions is due April 9.

Presentation: 10 Percent of the Project Grade

You will be asked to present your project in the last class. Although everyone is producing a written analysis as part of the final project, essays written for silent reading rarely work well as oral presentations. The presentation is intended to be an informal, five-minute presentation of the ideas that formed your final project. You will have to consider carefully how to best present your ideas to the class so that your thesis is clearly understood.

The criteria for evaluation is a clear and effective presentation of interesting ideas. This is due April 9.

Regulations on plagiarism and cheating will be strictly enforced in all stages of the project.

SCANLATION ASSIGNMENT (ARONSSON, FJORDEVIK, AND INOSE)
Before the Assignment

During the class time, the teacher explained the group work that is similar to scanlation. Most of the students knew what the scanlation was, but for those who did not know, the teacher explained how fans of Japanese manga would make its translation and distribute it. The teacher explained that in the assignment, the translated manga was not going be distributed but only shared within the class. The purpose of the exercise was to learn i) how to translate in cooperation with others, ii) how to translate manga, and iii) how to evaluate translation done by others (i.e., other groups). Then the students were asked to form groups of maximum four members, before the following class.

Preparation of the Material

The teacher translated the introductory chapter of the original material (*Shisso Nikki* by Hideo Azuma) and pasted the translated text next to the original, using the sticky note function of Adobe Reader. This chapter served as an example for the students of how to translate the rest of the chapters. Then the following instruction sheet was handed out to the students.

JP2005 Introduction to Translation
Group Work
The material is taken from the first part of 失踪日記（しっそうにっき, *Shissou Nikki* by Hideo Azuma, a work that has won various awards. It is a documentary work about a manga writer who is the author himself—how he virtually disappeared from his career and his family because of the work pressure.

Each group has two chapters (about eight pages per chapter) to translate. It is a serial, but each chapter could be read independently as well; however, you need to know the background, which is explained in the introductory chapter. I translated it myself (to check that it is not too difficult), so please have a look.

I used the sticky comment function of Adobe Reader, because it does not require the pro version of Adobe to use, and you can see both the original and the translation. However, if you would like to use some other function, you can. Please consult me.

As for the treatment of onomatopoeias, mimetic words, and names of shops (drawn within the frames), each group can discuss and decide what to do.

The translated version, in PDF format, should be ready by November 13. Each chapter should be in one file. Send the files to me by e-mail [e-mail address of the teacher included]. Then I will share them on the study platform Fronter, where you will read and comment on at least two other groups' chapters.

Please discuss and help one another to understand the text well. Determine the most appropriate tone of translation, the treatment of cultural terms, any onomatopoeias, and how to check the translation. You can decide how to divide the work as well (although I would like to know how you divided it).
Good luck!

All the groups had three weeks to translate assigned two chapters (sixteen pages in total) and upload it to FRONTER for the other groups to see. After the three weeks, the teacher instructed them to read and comment on a minimum of two chapters translated by other groups. The students studied the translation done by other groups, comparing the used translation strategies to their own translations, and made comments and suggestions for the improvement of translation.

BIBLIOGRAPHY

Abrahamson, Megan B. 2013. "J. R. R. Tolkien, Fanfiction, and the Freedom of the Reader." *Mythlore* 32 (1): 53–72.
Agbabi, Patience. 2015. *Telling Tales*. London: Canongate.
Allison, Paul. 2009. "Be a Blogger: Social Networking in the Classroom." In *Teaching the New Writing: Technology, Change, and Assessment in the 21st-century Classroom*, edited by Ann Herrington, Kevin Hodgson, and Charles Moran, 75–91. New York: Teachers College Press.
Anderson Howell, Katherine. 2014. "*Jane Eyre* Re-Written: Discourse, Remix, and Student Writing." *Pennsylvania English* 36: 7–19.
———. 2016. "Invitation vs. Intrusion: Contemplating the Ethics of Teaching Fan Methods." *Journal of Fandom Studies* 4 (3): 325–29.
Baker, Lucy. 2016. "Girl! Version: The Feminist Framework of Regendered Characters in Fanwork." *Journal of Fandom Studies* 4 (1): 23–36.
Baker-Whitelaw, Gavia. 2015. "What Not to Do When Teaching a Class about Fanfiction." Daily Dot, February 23. http://www.dailydot.com/irl/berkeley-fanfiction-class-backlash/.
Barry, Peter. 2002. *Beginning Theory: An Introduction to Literary and Cultural Theory*. Manchester, UK: Manchester University Press.
Bennett, Lucy. 2014. "Tracing *Textual Poachers*: Reflections on the Development of Fan Studies and Digital Fandom." *Journal of Fandom Studies* 2 (1): 5–20.
Bennett, Lucy, and Bertha Chin. 2014. "Exploring Fandom, Social Media, and Producer-Fan Interactions: An Interview with *Sleepy Hollow*'s Orlando Jones." *Transformative Works and Cultures* 17. http://dx.doi.org/10.3983/twc.2014.0601.
Biren, (Ratnesh) A. Nagda, Patricia Gurin, and Gretchen E. Lopez. 2003. "Transformative Pedagogy for Democracy and Social Justice." *Race Ethnicity and Education* 6 (2): 165–91.
Black, Rebecca W. 2008a. *Adolescents and Online Fan Fiction*. Vol. 23. New York: Peter Lang.

———. 2008b. "Convergence and Divergence: Informal Learning in Online Fanfiction Communities and Formal Writing Pedagogy." *Counterpoints* 338: 125–43.

———. 2009. "Online Fan Fiction, Global Identity, and Imagination." *Research in the Teaching of English* 43 (4): 397–425.

———. 2010. "Online Fan Fiction and Critical Media Literacy." *Journal of Computing in Teacher Education* 26 (2): 75–80.

Bledsoe, Glen L. 2009. "Collaborative Digital Writing: The Art of Writing Together Using Technology." In *Teaching the New Writing: Technology, Change, and Assessment in the 21st-Century Classroom*, edited by Ann Herrington, Kevin Hodgson, and Charles Moran, 39–54. New York: Teachers College Press.

Boler, Megan. 1999. *Feeling Power: Emotions and Education*. New York: Routledge.

Booth, Paul. 2010. *Digital Fandom: New Media Studies*. New York: Peter Lang.

———. 2012. "Fandom in the Classroom: A Pedagogy of Fan Studies." In *Fan Culture: Theory/Practice*, edited by Katherine Larsen and Lynn Zubernis, 174–87. Newcastle, UK: Cambridge Scholars Press.

———. 2013. "Augmenting Fan-Academic Dialogue: New Directions in Fan Research." *Journal of Fandom Studies* 1 (2): 119–37.

———. 2015a. "Fandom: The Classroom of the Future." *Transformative Works and Cultures* 19. http://dx.doi.org/10.3983/twc.2015.0650.

———. 2015b. *Game Play: Paratextuality in Contemporary Board Games*. New York: Bloomsbury.

———. 2015c. *Playing Fans: Negotiating Fandom and Media in the Digital Age*. Iowa City: University of Iowa Press.

Bouchard, Chris, dir. 2009. *The Hunt for Gollum*. Independent Online Cinema/Rickety Shack. http://www.thehuntforgollum.com/.

Burke, Amy. 2010. "A Visual Re-Telling of *The Seeress's Prophecy*." English 4401 performance, Mount Saint Vincent University, Halifax, NS, November 17. English 4401 essay, December 6.

Burns, Elizabeth, and Carlie Webber. 2009. "When Harry Met Bella: Fanfiction Is All the Rage. But Is It Plagiarism? Or the Perfect Thing to Encourage Young Writers?" *School Library Journal* 55 (8): 26–29.

Busse, Kristina. 2013. "Geek Hierarchies, Boundary Policing, and the Gendering of the Good Fan." *Participations* 10 (1): 73–91.

Busse, Kristina, and Karen Hellekson, eds. 2006. *Fan Fiction and Fan Communities in the Age of the Internet: New Essays*. Jefferson, NC: McFarland.

———. 2012. "Identity, Ethics, and Fan Privacy." In *Fan Culture: Theory/Practice*, edited by Katherine Larsen and Lynn Zubernis, 38–56. Newcastle, UK: Cambridge Scholars.

Busse, Kristina, Alexis Lothian, and Robin Anne Reid. 2007. "'Yearning Void and Infinite Potential': Online Slash Fandom as Queer Female Space." *English Language Notes* 45 (2): 103–11.

Centrumlumina. 2013. "AO3 Census: Masterpost." Tumblr, May 10. http://centrumlumina.tumblr.com/post/63208278796/ao3-census-masterpost.

Collins, Suzanne. 2008. *The Hunger Games*. New York: Scholastic Press.

Coppa, Francesca. 2006. "Writing Bodies in Space: Media Fan Fiction as Theatrical Performance." In *Fan Fiction and Fan Communities in the Age of the Internet: New Essays*, edited by Karen Hellekson and Kristina Busse, 225–44. Jefferson, NC: McFarland.

———. 2008. "Women, *Star Trek*, and the Early Development of Fannish Vidding." *Transformative Works and Cultures* 1. http://journal.transformativeworks.org/index.php/twc/article/view/44.

———. 2014. "Fuck Yeah, Fandom Is Beautiful." *Journal of Fandom Studies* 2 (1): 73–82.

Curwood, Jenn Scott, Alecia Marie Magnifico, and Jayne C. Lammers. 2013. "Writing in the Wild: Writers' Motivation in Fan-Based Affinity Spaces." *Journal of Adolescent and Adult Literacy* 56 (8) 677–85.

Dale, Edgar. 1969. *Audio-Visual Methods in Teaching*. 3rd ed. New York: Holt, Rinehart and Winston.

Darabont, Frank, dir. 1994. *The Shawshank Redemption*. Castle Rock Entertainment.

Davison, Jenny. 2011. "Design Log." English 4401 assignment, Mount Saint Vincent University, Halifax, NS, April 21.

Dech, Emily. 2015. "Renovation Commences for Reformatory's Penal Museum." *Richland Source* 8. http://www.richlandsource.com/life_and_culture/renovation-commences-for-reformatory-s-penal-museum/article_31fccf9e-96af-11e4-86c2-df2006e6591c.html.

De Kosnik, Abigail. 2009. "Should Fan Fiction Be Free?" *Cinema Journal* 48 (4): 118–24.

Derrida, Jacques. 2001. "Structure, Sign and Play in the Discourse of the Human Sciences." In *Modern Literary Theory*, 4th ed., edited by Philip Rice and Patricia Waugh, 194–209. New York: Oxford University Press.

Deuze, Mark. 2012. *Media Life*. Cambridge, UK: Polity Press.

Duffett, Mark. 2015. "Fan Practices." *Popular Music and Society* 38 (no. 1): 1–6.

Eagleton, Terry. 1986. *Against the Grain: Essays, 1975–1985*. London: Verso, 1986.

Elbow, Peter. 1997. "High Stakes and Low Stakes in Assigning and Responding to Writing." *New Directions for Teaching and Learning* 69: 5–13.

Ford, Sam. 2014. "Fan Studies: Grappling with an 'Undisciplined' Discipline." *Journal of Fandom Studies* 2 (1): 53–71.

Freire, Paulo. 1970. *Pedagogy of the Oppressed*. New York: Continuum.

Freund, Katharina. 2010. "I'm Glad We Got Burned, Think of All the Things We Learned": Fandom Conflict and Context in Counteragent's "Still Alive." *Transformative Works and Cultures* 4. http://dx.doi.org/10.3983/twc.2010.0187.

Gardner, John. 1989. *Grendel*. New York: Vintage Books.

Gaston, Sarah, and Robin Anne Reid. 2012. "Race and Ethnicity in Fandom." *Transformative Works and Cultures* 8. http://dx.doi.org/10.3983/twc.2012.0392.

Gee, James Paul. 2005. "Semiotic Social Spaces and Affinity Spaces: From *The Age of Mythology* to Today's Schools." In *Beyond Communities of Practice: Language, Power, and Social Context*, edited by David Barton and Karin Tusting, 214–32. Cambridge, UK: Cambridge University Press.

Gee, James Paul, and Elisabeth R. Hayes. 2011. *Language and Learning in the Digital Age*. New York: Routledge.

George, Nelson. 2011. "'The Help,' Hollywood's Movie on Civil Rights Era." *New York Times*, August 9. http://www.nytimes.com/2011/08/14/movies/black-and-white-struggle-through-hollywoods-rosy-glow.html.

Geraghty, Lincoln. 2012. "Just Who Is the Passive Audience Here? Teaching Fan Studies at University." In *Fan Culture: Theory/Practice*, edited by Katherine Larsen and Lynn Zubernis, 162–73. Newcastle, UK: Cambridge Scholars Press.

———. 2014. *Cult Collectors*. London, UK: Routledge.

Gnanadass, Edith. 2014. "Learning to Teach about Race." *Adult Learning* 25 (3): 96–102.

Gray, Jonathan, C. Lee Harrington, and Cornel Sandvoss, eds. 2007. *Fandom: Identities and Communities in a Mediated World*. New York: New York University Press.

Gray-Rosendale, Laura, and Kendra Birnley. 2011. "Reconfiguring Differences: Radicalizing Popular Culture Pedagogy." In *Queer Popular Culture: Literature, Media, Film and Television*, edited by Thomas Peele, 215–27. Gordonsville, US: Palgrave Macmillan.

Gutiérrez, Peter. 2011. "The Right to Be a Fan." *Language Arts* 88 (3): 226–31.

Haltinner, Kristin. 2016. *Teaching Race and Anti-Racism in Contemporary America*. New York: Springer.

Heit, Jamey. 2015. *The Politics of the Hunger Games*. Jefferson, NC: McFarland.

Hellekson, Karen. 2009. "A Fannish Field of Value: Online Fan Gift Culture." *Cinema Journal* 48 (4): 113–18. http://dx.doi.org/10.1353/cj.0.0140.

Hellekson, Karen, and Kristina Busse, eds. 2006. *Fan Fiction and Fan Communities in the Age of the Internet: New Essays*. Jefferson, NC: McFarland.

Herritt, Jessica. 2013. "Tolkien's Use of Binary Structure." English 4475 performance, Mount Saint Vincent University, Halifax, NS, November 27.

Hill, Logan. 2007. "The Vidder." *New York*, November 12. http://nymag.com/movies/features/videos/40622/.

Hills, Matt. 2002. *Fan Cultures*. Abingdon, UK: Taylor & Francis. http://www.tandfebooks.com/action/showBook?doi=10.4324/9780203361337.

———. 2012. "'Twilight' Fans Represented in Commercial Paratexts and Inter-Fandoms: Resisting and Repurposing Negative Fan Stereotypes." In *Genre, Reception, and Adaptation in the Twilight Series*, edited by Anne Morew, 113–29. Burlington, VT: Ashgate.

———. 2014a. "*Doctor Who*'s Textual Commemorators: Fandom, Collective Memory and the Self-Commodification of Fanfac." *Journal of Fandom Studies* 2 (1): 31–51.

———. 2014b. "From Dalek Half Balls to Daft Punk Helmets: Mimetic Fandom and the Crafting of Replicas." *Transformative Works and Cultures* 16. http://dx.doi.org/10.3983/ twc.2014.0531.

Holmes, Anna. 2012. "White until Proven Black: Imagining Race in Hunger Games." *New Yorker*, March 30. http://www.newyorker.com/books/page-turner/white-until-proven-black-imagining-race-in-hunger-games.

"Honors Program Current Courses." 2016. Ashland, February 26. https://www.ashland.edu/administration/honors-program/current-courses.

Huddleston, Kathie. 2002. "In an Exclusive Interview, Writer/Producer Joss Whedon Talks about His Upcoming Series—FIREFLY." Scifi. https://web.archive.org/web/20021012090222/www.scifi.com/scifimag/october2002/transcripts.

Hutcheon, Linda, with Siobhan O'Flynn. 2013. *A Theory of Adaptation*. 2nd ed. London: Routledge.

Inose, Hiroko. 2012. "Scanlation: What Fan Translators of Manga Learn in the Informal Learning Environment." *International Symposium of Language and Communication* 6: 73–83.

Jackson, Drew. 2014. "Design Log Part 2." English 4475 assignment, Mount Saint Vincent University, Halifax, NS, March 26.

Jackson, Peter, dir. 2001–2003. *The Lord of the Rings: The Fellowship of the Ring; The Two Towers; The Return of the King*. Film trilogy. New Line Cinema.

Jamison, Anne. 2013. *Fic: Why Fanfiction Is Taking over the World*. Dallas, TX: BenBella Books.

Jenkins, Henry. 1992. *Textual Poachers: Television Fans and Participatory Culture*. New York: Routledge.

———. 2006a. *Convergence Culture: Where Old and New Media Collide*. New York: New York University Press.

———. 2006b. *Confronting the Challenges of Participatory Culture: Media Education for the 21st Century*. Chicago: MacArthur Foundation.

———. 2006c. *Fans, Bloggers and Gamers: Exploring Participatory Culture*. New York: New York University Press.

———. 2010. *TEDxNYED*. YouTube video. https://youtube/AFCLKaoXRlw.

———. n.d. "Who the &%&# is Henry Jenkins?: Aca/Fan Defined." *Confessions of an Aca-Fan*. http://henryjenkins.org/aboutmehtml/.

Jenkins, Henry, Sam Ford, and Joshua Green. 2013. *Spreadable Media: Creating Value and Meaning in a Networked Culture*. New York: New York University Press.

Johnson, Derek. 2007. "Fan-tagonism: Factions, Institutions, and Constitutive Hegemonies of Fandom." In *Fandom: Identities and Communities in a Mediated World*, edited by Jonathan Gray, C. Lee Harrington, and Cornell Sandvoss, 285–300. New York: New York University Press.

Kell, Tracey. 2009. "Using Fan Fiction to Teach Critical Reading and Writing Skills." *Teacher Librarian* 37 (1): 32–35.

King, Stephen. 1982. *Rita Hayworth and Shawshank Redemption: A Story from Different Seasons*. Thorndike, ME: Thorndike Press.

Kolb, David A. 1984. *Experiential Learning: Experience as the Source of Learning and Development*. New York: Prentice Hall.

Lancaster, Kurt. 2001. *Interacting with Babylon 5: Fan Performances in a Media Universe*. Austin, TX: University of Texas Press.

Larsen, Katherine, and Lynn Zubernis, eds. 2012. *Fan Culture: Theory/Practice*. Newcastle, UK: Cambridge Scholars Press.

Lessig, Lawrence. 2008. *Remix: Making Art and Commerce Thrive in the Hybrid Economy*. New York: Penguin.

Lévy, Pierre. 1997. *Collective Intelligence: Mankind's Emerging World in Cyberspace*. Cambridge, UK: Perseus.

Liston, Daniel P., and Sirat Al Salim. 2002. "Race, Discomfort, and Love in a University Classroom." In *Race in the College Classroom: Pedagogy and Politics*, edited by Bonnie TuSmith and Maureen T. Reddy, 239–52. New Brunswick, NJ: Rutgers University Press.

MacGregor, Shelby. 2015. "An Imagined Dystopian *LotR* Film." *A Single Leaf*. Anna Smol, January 9. https://annasmol.net/2015/01/09/an-imagined-dystopian-lotr-film/.

Martin, Kathleen J. 2010. "Student Attitudes and the Teaching and Learning of Race, Culture and Politics." *Teaching and Teacher Education* 26 (3): 530–39. http://dx.doi.org/10.1016/j.tate.2009.06.018.

Martin, Mary C. 2015. "Service Learning as Marketing Pedagogy: Practical, Theoretical, and Institutional Perspectives." *Academy of Educational Leadership Journal* 19 (2): 109–27. https://www.researchgate.net/publication/292145565_Service_Learning_as_Marketing_Pedagogy_Practical_Theoretical_and_Institutional_Perspectives.

McIntosh, Peggy. 1990. "White Privilege: Unpacking the Invisible Knapsack." *Independent School* 49 (2): 31–35.

Mikhaylova, Larisa. 2012. "Star Trek film (2009) and Russian SF Fandom: Too Many Batteries Included." In *Fan Culture: Theory/Practice*, edited by Katherine Larsen and Lynn Zubernis, 148–61. Newcastle, UK: Cambridge Scholars.

Mongan, Shelby. 2015. "Finding Truth in Playing Pretend: A Reflection on Cosplay." *Transformative Works and Cultures* 18. http://journal.transformativeworks.org/index.php/twc/article/view/634/481.

Morimoto, Lori, and Bertha Chin. 2013. "Towards a Theory of Transcultural Fandom." *Participations* 10 (1): 92–108.

Nielsen, E. J. 2016. "Dear Researcher: Rethinking Engagement with Fan Authors." *Journal of Fandom Studies* 4 (3): 233–49.

Olin-Scheller, Christina, and Patrik Wikström. 2010. *Författande fans*. Lund, Sweden: Studentlitteratur.

Pande, Rukmini. 2016. "Squee from the Margins: Racial/Cultural/Ethnic Identity in Global Media Fandom." In *Seeing Fans*, edited by Paul Booth and Lucy Bennett, 209–20. New York: Bloomsbury.

Penley, Constance. 1992. "Cultural Studies." In *Feminism, Psychoanalysis, and the Study of Popular Culture*, edited by Lawrence Grossberg, Cary Nelson, and Paula Treichler, 479–500. New York: Routledge.

Perez, Nistasha. 2013. "Gif Fics and the Rebloggable Canon of SuperWhoLock." In *Fan Phenomena: Doctor Who*, edited by Paul Booth, 148–57. Bristol, UK: Intellect.

Pharr, Mary F., Leisa A. Clark, Donald E. Palumbo, and C. W. Sullivan III. 2012. *Of Bread, Blood, and* The Hunger Games: *Critical Essays on the Suzanne Collins Trilogy*. Jefferson, NC: McFarland.

Phillips, Leah. 2013. "Design Log." English 4475 assignment, Mount Saint Vincent University, Halifax, NS, November 13.

Power, Rebecca. 2014. "Tolkien's Alliterative Meter and a Reproduction of 'Of Beren and Lúthien.'" English 4475 assignment, Mount Saint Vincent University, Halifax, NS, April 13.

Pugh, Sheenagh. 2005. *The Democratic Genre: Fan Fiction in a Literary Context*. Bridgend, UK: Seren.

Roberson, Richard Jr., and Maura Grady. 2015. "The Shawshank Trail: A Cross-Disciplinary Study in Film-Induced Tourism and Fan Culture." *Almatourism: Journal of Tourism, Culture and Territorial Development* 6 (4): 47–66. http://almatourism.unibo.it/article/view/4953.

Säljö, Roger. 2000. *Lärande i praktiken: Ett sociokulturellt perspektiv*. Stockholm: Norstedts.

———. 2004. "Learning and Technologies, People and Tools in Coordinated Activities." *International Journal of Educational Research* 41: 489–94.

———. 2015. *Lärande. En introduktion till perspektiv och metaforer*. Malmö, Sweden: Gleerups.

Säljö, Roger, Ulf P. Lundgren, and Caroline Liberg, ed. 2014. *Lärande, skola, bildning*. 3rd ed. Edited by Roger Säljö, Ulf P. Lundgren, and Caroline Liberg. Stockholm: Natur & Kultur.

Schmidt, Lisa. 2010. "Monstrous Melodrama: Expanding the Scope of Melodramatic Identification to Interpret Negative Fan Responses to *Supernatural*." *Transformative Works and Cultures* 4. http://dx.doi.org/10.3983/twc.2010.0152.

Scott, Damien. 2012. "The 25 Most Racist Tweets about 'The Hunger Games.'" Complex, March 28. http://www.complex.com/pop-culture/2012/03/the-25-most-racist-tweets-about-the-hunger-games/.

Scott, Suzanne. 2009. "Repackaging Fan Culture: The Regifting Economy of Ancillary Content Models." *Transformative Works and Cultures* 3. http://dx.doi.org/10.3983/twc.2009.0150.

Shawshank Redemption and Lady Justice. 2010. YouTube video. https://youtube/Z61WMUICATI.

stannisbarathenon. 2013. "Live-Action Modern-Day 'The Lion King.'" Tumblr. http://stannisbaratheon.tumblr.com/post/58498886405/live-action-modern-day-the-lion-king-new-york.

Stedman, Kyle D. 2012. "Remix Literacy and Fan Compositions." *Computers and Composition* 29 (2): 107–23. http://dx.doi.org/10.1016/j.compcom.2012.02.002.

Stein, Louisa Ellen, and Kristina Busse. 2012. *Sherlock and Transmedia Fandom: Essays on the BBC Series*. Jefferson, NC: McFarland.

Terranova, Tiziana. 2003. "Free Labor: Producing Culture for the Digital Economy." *Electronic Book Review*, June 20. http://www.electronicbookreview.com/thread/technocapitalism/voluntary.

Tolkien, J. R. R. 1979. *The Silmarillion*, edited by Christopher Tolkien. London: HarperCollins.

———. 1981. *The Letters of J. R. R. Tolkien*, edited by Humphrey Carpenter and Christopher Tolkien. London: George Allen & Unwin.

———. 1994. *The Lord of the Rings*. Boston: Houghton Mifflin.

———. 2008. *Tolkien on Fairy-Stories: Expanded Edition, with Commentary and Notes*, edited by Verlyn Flieger and Douglas A. Anderson. New York: HarperCollins.

Turk, Tisha, and Joshua Johnson. 2012. "Toward an Ecology of Vidding." *Transformative Works and Cultures* 9. http://dx.doi.org/10.3983/twc.2012.0326.

Turner, Cory. 2011. "On Location: Mansfield, Ohio's 'Shawshank Industry." *All Things Considered*. NPR, August 4. http://www.npr.org/2011/08/04/138986482/on-location-mansfield-ohios-shawshank-industry.

Zemeckis, Robert, dir. 2007. *Beowulf*. Paramount Pictures.

Zubernis, Lynn, and Katherine Larsen. 2012. *Fandom at the Crossroads: Celebration, Shame and Fan-Producer Relationships*. Newcastle, UK: Cambridge Scholars Press.

CONTRIBUTORS

Katherine Anderson Howell is an independent scholar and multigenre writer who lives in Washington, DC. She taught academic writing at the college level for eleven years, including a course in rewriting canonical literature. Her poems can be found in *On the Issues, Riveter Review, Gargoyle, Snapdragon: A Journal of Arts and Healing, The Way to My Heart: An Anthology of Food-Related Romance*, and are forthcoming in *Beach Reads 2: Lost and Found*. Her academic work is available in *Pennsylvania English, Inside Higher Ed*, the *Journal of Fandom Studies*, and *Media Commons*. Her essays have been published on The Rumpus and Cold Takes websites and in *Women in Higher Education*. Her research interests include the influence of *Jane Eyre* on contemporary female heroines; sexually explicit student writing and classroom trigger warnings; and remix pedagogy.

Mattias Aronsson is an associate professor of French at Dalarna University in Sweden, where he teaches French and didactics. His main research areas are contemporary French and Swedish literature (twentieth and twenty-first centuries), and his interests include the fields of cultural studies, reader response studies, postcolonial studies, and translation studies. He presented his doctoral dissertation, "La thématique de l'eau dans l'œuvre de Marguerite Duras," at Göteborg University in 2006, and he has published articles and book chapters on the works of Marguerite Duras, Faïza Guène, and Vilhelm Ekelund.

Paul Booth is associate professor of communication at DePaul University in Chicago. He is the author of *Playing Fans: Negotiating Fandom and Media in the Digital Age* (University of Iowa Press, 2015), *Game Play: Paratextuality in Contemporary Board Games* (Bloomsbury, 2015), *Digital Fandom: New Media Studies* (Peter Lang, 2010), and *Time on TV: Temporal Displacement and Mashup*

Television (Peter Lang, 2012) as well as the editor of *Fan Phenomena: Doctor Who* (Intellect, 2013), *Seeing Fans: Representations of Fandom in Media and Popular Culture* (with Lucy Bennett, Bloomsbury, 2016), *and Controversies in Digital Ethics* (with Amber Davisson, Bloomsbury, 2016).

Shannon K. Farley has successfully defended her dissertation in support of her PhD in comparative literature at the University of Massachusetts at Amherst. She also holds a terminal master's in comparative literature from UMass, and she earned her bachelor's degree at Williams College in history and classics. She gave a presentation at Vividcon 2014 on the topic of this chapter, and she has been published in *Transformative Works and Cultures* as well as in *M/C* in an article she cowrote with Kristina Busse.

Anneli Fjordevik is a senior lecturer in German at Dalarna University in Sweden, where she teaches German literature. She has written articles and teaching materials in the fields of intertextuality, intermediality, and women's writing around 1800 in German literature and is part of a project about interactivity in digital literature in the German-speaking world. She presented her doctoral dissertation, "Heinrich von Kleists Amphitryon. Ein Lustspiel nach Molière unter dem Aspekt der Intertextualität im Gesamtwerk," at Uppsala University in 2004.

Erika Gallion is a 2014 graduate of Ashland University in Ohio, where she majored in English and creative writing. She is also a 2016 graduate of Kent State University, where she received a master's of education in higher education administration and student affairs. Currently Erika works for the University of North Florida in Jacksonville as a study abroad advisor. She recently started working on a master of arts degree in literature.

Maura Grady is the director of composition and an assistant professor of English at Ashland University. She is the author of several publications on film, television, and fan culture, including "From Work to Text: Reading *The Raven Waits* as Beowulf Fan Fiction." She is also a coauthor of "Nostalgia for Empire: *Doctor Who*, 1963–74" and "The Shawshank Trail: A Cross-Disciplinary Study in Film-Induced Tourism and Fan Culture" in *Almatourism: Journal of Tourism, Culture, and Territorial Development*. Portions of that article appear in this book.

Lee Hibbard is a PhD candidate in the rhetoric and composition program at Purdue University. His research interests include the rhetoric of fandom spaces, digital texts, and queer rhetorics, and he is currently studying queer fandom communities and representation in video games while teaching first-year composition. He is also a staff writer for *Not Your Mama's Gamer*.

Hiroko Inose is a senior lecturer in Japanese at Dalarna University in Sweden and a visiting lecturer at Granada University in Spain, where she teaches Japanese language, translation, literature, and popular culture. Her main research interests are translation studies (literature/manga translation) and Japanese popular culture (especially anime and manga). She presented her doctoral thesis, "La Traducción de Onomatopeyas y Mímesis Japonesas al Español y al Inglés: Los Casos de la Novela y el Manga," at Granada University in 2009.

Ashlyn Keefe graduated with a master of arts in media and cinema studies from DePaul University in Chicago in 2014, where her main areas of interest were complex narratives in television and film, fan studies, and Iranian cinema. She currently works as a copywriter in Chicago and spends all of her free time horseback riding, seeing movies, and watching far too much television.

Leslie Leonard recently completed her master's of English at the University of Alabama in Huntsville and started a doctoral program on American literature in the fall of 2017. She is currently researching the productivity and performativity of machines in the nineteenth century and the ways in which nineteenth-century mechanization manifests in the creative works of the period.

Rukmini Pande completed her PhD on Intersections of Identity in Media Fandom Communities at the University of Western Australia and currently is an assistant professor at O.P. Jindal Global University. She serves on the editorial board of the *Journal of Fandom Studies* and has been published in multiple edited collections on Race in Media Fandom, including *Seeing Fans* (edited by Paul Booth and Lucy Bennett) and in *Fic: Why Fanfiction Is Taking Over the World* (edited by Anne Jamison). Additionally, she has co-authored an article, "'Yes, the Evil Queen Is Latina!': Racial Dynamics of Online Femslash Fandoms" in a special issue of the journal *Transformative Works and Cultures* (June 2017). Her dissertation is also under contract to be published as a monograph with the University of Iowa Press.

Rebecca Power graduated from Mount Saint Vincent University in May 2015 with a bachelor's degree in English. Her honors thesis focused on J. R. R. Tolkien's story of Beren and Lúthien and his use of Old English–style alliterative meter in modern English. As part of her thesis she included an adaptation of Beren and Lúthien written in alliterative verse. As a creative and academic writer she has presented both poetry and academic papers at the annual Atlantic Undergraduate English Conference and has read her poetry at campus events. Rebecca is attending graduate school to pursue her passion for English and creative writing with the goal of obtaining a master's and a PhD in English.

Richard J. "Robby" Roberson Jr. is an assistant professor of management in the School of Business and Public Management at the Coastal College of Georgia in Brunswick, Georgia. He is the coauthor of "The Shawshank Trail: A Cross-Disciplinary Study in Film-Induced Tourism and Fan Culture."

John Sanders graduated from the University of Massachusetts at Amherst in 2014 with a bachelor's degree in comparative literature with an individualized concentration in game scholarship. He is continuing his research into games, literature, and new media as an English PhD student at Syracuse University, exploring screen culture as both a student and an instructor. He often finds himself on YouTube in his "spare" time and still watches the occasional vid.

Anna Smol is a professor of English literature at Mount Saint Vincent University in Halifax, Nova Scotia, Canada, where she teaches courses on medieval literature, medievalism, and Tolkien. She is the recipient of her university's Alumnae Award for Teaching Excellence and the University Instructional Leadership Award. She has published and presented on J. R. R. Tolkien, children's literature, medievalism, fandom, and Old English poetry as well as on teaching and learning, including an article in *MLA Approaches to Teaching Tolkien's* Lord of the Rings *and Other Works*. Her website and blog can be found at http://annasmol.net.

Yixian Yang is a senior human resources major from China. She is an only child and came to the University of Alabama in Huntsville in order to become more confident and independent. She found it difficult to adapt to the new environment and education model, but she is excited by the friends that she has made and by the things that she has learned while studying there.

Lingzi "Lindsey" Yuan is a transfer student from China and a senior accounting major studying at the University of Alabama in Huntsville. While taking the English 101 writing class in which the research was conducted, Lindsey was also experiencing her first year in the United States and was unaccustomed to but passionate about the new learning style. She is now preparing for graduation and for entrance to graduate school. The schools that she is applying to require essays, but after taking three writing courses in the past two years of her studies, Lindsey feels confident in her essay-writing ability.

INDEX

academic writing, 48
acafan, 31, 116–17, 128
adaptation, 19–20
affinity: space, 51–52; based-learning, 70; space learning, 123
anonymity: on Tumblr, 55, 60–61; impact on grading, 79
antiracist pedagogy, 101–5
assignment, 21, 74–77, 106–7; exercise, 71–73
autoethnography, 121–23

beta reader, 60, 79
Black, Rebecca, 51; discussion of *Critical Media Literacy*, 48, 62
blog, 51; in student culture, 63–64, 67
Booth, Paul, 26, 30

canonical, 17; online engagement with, 48
collaboration: in fan spaces, 48, 52; in scanlation, 78–81
composition, 54, 65
consent: in research, 41; sexual desire, 88
Coppa, Francesca, 27, 83
cosplay, 19
creativity, 18–19; grading creative work, 27; in language learning, 70–73; in vidding, 94

deconstruction, 84–85, 94
Derrida, Jacques, 84–85
discomfort, 90, 94, 98, 102, 104, 110
discourse, 120; fan work as resistant to, 101

English as a Second Language (ESL), 58, 66, 67–69
ethics: in research, 41; teaching fan works, 97, 122–23

fan communities, 53, 70, 106, 123; creating nonprofit entities, 36; norms, 19–20; whiteness and race in, 98, 110
fan fiction, 27, 31, 54, 65, 71–74
fan pilgrimage. *See* film-induced tourism
fan studies, 41, 97, 101, 114–16
fan vids. *See* vids
fan work, 20, 28, 83, 98, 122
fandom, 26, 39, 96, 119, 124; *Supernatural*, 90
film-induced tourism, 38; fan wariness, 46
Firefly, 91–92
foreign language teaching, 80–81

gender, 92, 98
genderbending, 99
genre, 21; slash, 119
Geraghty, Lincoln, 115, 116, 124
gif (graphic interchange format), 58; gif-set, 99
grading, 27, 28, 79, 81
Gray, Jonathan, C. Lee Harrington, and Cornel Sandvoss, 115, 122

hashtags, 57–59
Hills, Matt: student response to, 39; on autoethnography, 121
human research, 41
Hunger Games, The, 100

167

Hutcheon, Linda, 18–19

informal writing, 48–49, 53, 56, 65
institutional review board, 41
interdisciplinary, 29, 43, 45, 96–97
intertextuality, 54; in medievalism, 17–19

Jenkins, Henry, 117, 122; contrast with other views of fandom, 118

language learning, 71–72, 75–77
Lion King, The, 101; assignment, 107
Livejournal (acafan participation), 52, 90
Lord of the Rings, 21, 22
low-stakes assignment, 48, 56, 57

manga, 70; *Shissou Nikki*, 74–75; student reaction, 77–78
market research, 37, 40, 43
media text, 104, 116
meta, 20, 115
misogyny, 90
mobile fan community, 35

online culture, 62
online education. *See* web-based courses
online seminar, 71, 81
online writing, 48, 50, 54; peer-review, 49, 61; English as a Second Language students, 58

participation, 45, 49, 96
participatory culture, 52, 97–98, 114, 122
participatory learning, 107
pedagogy: informal, 70; fan works in, 96; critical race, 102; fan studies, 114. *See also* antiracist pedagogy
peer review, 51, 56, 61, 68, 73–74, 79

play, 20, 28, 127
popular culture, 100–101, 108, 114–20
privacy, 4, 97, 122

race, 98, 100
racebending, 99, 110; assignment, 107
racism, 102; in media texts, 104
racist, 91–92
rigor: low stakes assignments, 56; emotion, 124

scanlation, 70, 75–77
scholar-fan, 125. *See also* acafan
service learning, 35, 46
sexuality, 101, 110, 119
slash, 86–87, 119–20
social media, 42, 50–51; guidance for instructor, 54; using personal devices, 59
storytelling, 18, 32, 43

The Shawshank Trail, 36
transformative, 18, 97; learning, 109
transmedia, 29
Tumblr, 38, 55–62, 98

University of California, Berkeley, fan fiction course, 19, 97, 123

vidding, 83–84
vids, 84; ecology of, 87; *Handlebars*, 85; *How Much is that Geisha In the Window?*, 91–92; *Telephone*, 88–89; *Tonight I'm F—cking You*, 87–88; *Whole New Way*, 86–87; *Women's Work*, 89–90; *Women's Work* as pedagogical tool, 90

web-based courses, 70
white privilege, 102, 105, 108